Let me take you down,
'cause I'm going to Strawberry Fields.
Nothing is real
and nothing to get hung about.
Strawberry Fields forever.
Strawberry Fields forever.

STRAWBERRY FIELDS FOREVER:
JOHN LENNON REMEMBERED

by Vic Garbarini and Brian Cullman
with Barbara Graustark

Special Introduction by Dave Marsh

A Delilah Book

A BANTAM BOOK
NEW YORK • TORONTO • LONDON

STRAWBERRY FIELDS FOREVER: JOHN LENNON REMEMBERED
A Delilah Book | A Bantam Book | December 1980

ISBN 0-553-20121-2

Bantam Books are published by Bantam Books, Inc. Its trademark, consisting of the words "Bantam Books" and the por-
trayal of a bantam, is registered in the United States Patent
Office and in other countries. Marca Registrada. Bantam
Books, Inc., 666 Fifth Avenue, New York, New York 10103.

ACKNOWLEDGMENTS

Editorial Assistants: Mark Mehler, Roy Trakin

Researcher: Larry Joseph

For Delilah: Stephanie Bennett and Jeannie Sakol

Special Thanks to: Joan Tarshish, Clodagh Symons, Karen Moline, Madeleine Morel, Barbara Alpert, Julie Moline, and Mary Jane Lunn

CONTENTS

INTRODUCTION
BY DAVE MARSH

The talk we've heard since John Lennon's death emphasizes his career as Beatle, musician, father, artist, husband, symbol. This is fitting in a time of mourning, but it does not begin to take the measure of the man we lost.

John Lennon lived in exceptional times and he was one of the figures who made them exceptional—not because he had such immense musical gifts, or functioned as a youth leader, or brought intellectuality to rock and roll, or because he had the instinctive sense of how to rock his (and your) ass off. These were replaceable qualities. If Lennon had not been a rocker, other men would have made his breakthroughs, other men would have written similar songs. History says that this is inevitable, that process makes the world, not great men.

What great men own that process cannot claim is courage and heart. What set John Lennon apart was his bravery, not just in challenging the Vietnam War or in forcing anyone with half-a-brain to understand that the Beatles had really broken up, or in insisting that the ideals of peace and love on which his later work was founded could never grow outmoded. He had, for one thing, the courage to stand by a woman he loved when all around her were mocking her race and her ideas, her figure and her influence over him. Say what you will, it is only in the last few days that the world has discovered the great heart of Yoko Ono. It is a tribute to John Lennon that he knew it all along.

Together with Yoko, John determined to make his life have meaning, to take the celebrity which descended upon him like a plague and turn it to his own purposes. This calls for stamina and another kind of bravery, the willingness to spurn not false riches but false adulation and to challenge its errors every step of the way. John Lennon did this in his public life and he did it more than ever in retreat, and he applied what he learned not only to his judgment of the world but, as those who read Barbara Graustark's interview will quickly see, to himself as well.

What John Lennon would have eventually made of the society in which he was cut down, no one can say. One can be certain that his killing is a product of a nasty time in which the forces of repression are moving to choke off the living essences which he was just beginning to contact again. And that he would have fought that society, struggled to change it, groped to understand why it was happening now.

The loss of such a man as this is worth mourning. But it is also a sign that all of us need to rededicate ourselves, to begin to ask hard questions once again about our lives of casual cruelty and pettiness. For it is only in that context that John Lennon could have been shot, it is only in this way that we can honor him in our mourning. And it is only thus that we can prevent such foul murder from ever occurring again.

December, 1980

1

THE DREAM IS OVER

Years ago, I heard of a man who went to the movie
Ben Hur every day, often staying for several showings.
Between shows, he would stand in the lobby and make
bets on who would win the chariot race, always betting
on the charioteer whose wheel loosened and came off,
sending his chariot crashing into the bleachers.

"Why does the wheel always come off?" he kept
saying. "Eventually it's got to change, it'll stay on, and
he'll win the race."

I began to understand him the week of John Lennon's death.

On the Thursday after the murder, I was still buying
every paper—the *New York Times,* several editions of
the *New York Post,* the *New York Daily News* and
Tonight, News World, as well as copies of the *Washington Post,* the *Boston Globe,* the *San Francisco
Chronicle*—in what I realize now was the hope that if I
finally bought the right paper, the news would change,
it would all have been a mistake: the wheel would stay
on the chariot, John Lennon would be alive and well. I
never found the newspaper.

The news remained the same:

John Lennon, former member of the Beatles, was
shot to death at 10:50 p.m. Monday outside his
apartment on West 72d Street and Central Park

West. Lennon, 40, was taken to Roosevelt Hospital where he was pronounced dead at 11:15 p.m. Police said a suspect has been taken into custody.

Most events, at least most public events, are folded into time—the world stops for a moment, and then, a moment later, the world continues. This event refused to fold, and the people who were shaken on Monday night and Tuesday morning, when the news invaded all of our lives, continued to be shaken and hurt and confused. The pain did not stop and the fact did not go away: John Lennon was dead.

A fuse had blown out in our lives, and we stumbled around in the dark, bumping into each other in ways we had almost forgotten. For a while, in that global village of the sixties, we seemed to breathe with the Beatles, and by virtue of their very existence, we all seemed to breathe the same breath. Within an hour of the release of a new Beatles song, everyone in the world, or in a particular world, heard it, knew it, assimilated it. We all listened to the same radio. Monday night, we all listened to the same radio again: the community that had fragmented and disintegrated was suddenly reunited, but this time the radio was playing a different song.

This was not simply another casualty of life in the fast lane, one more rock-and-roll lunatic gone to drugs, drink, or despair. It was an assassination. That word, reserved for kings and queens and presidents, was the only one that fit.

In the anger and pain of the moment, it was hard to remember exactly who and what had died—the sheer volume of history, love, and associations was (and remains) staggering. But what was clear was that to a great many people all over the world, Lennon meant more than kings or queens or presidents.

John Lennon held out hope. He imagined, and however quietistic he became, he never lost that Utopian identification. But when you hold out hope people get real disappointed if you can't deliver. You're famous and they're not—that's the crux of your relationship. You command the power they crave—the power to make one's identity felt in the world, to be known. No matter that you're even further from resolving anyone's perplexities than the next bohemian, artist, or intellectual. You're denying your most desperate admirers the release they need, and a certain percentage of them will resent or hate you for it. From there, it only takes one to kill.

—Robert Christgau
Village Voice
Dec. 10, 1980

That one person showed up Monday night, December 8, in the form of Mark David Chapman.

For a few hours late Monday night and into Tuesday morning, before the "suspect's" name was released, I hoped they'd leave him anonymous and not give him whatever solace or satisfaction might exist in fame. After all, I can't remember the name of every president of the U.S., but I know the name Lee Harvey Oswald. But the name was released, and instead of some international conspiracy or age-old vendetta being worked out, the killer turned out to be some twisted, pathetic, scared kid from Hawaii, a casualty case who'd bought a gun and borrowed some money, who idolized Lennon, who got Lennon's autograph just hours before he shot him there, outside the Dakota, and who signed off work (on October 23, just before he left Hawaii) under the name John Lennon.

I am he
as you are he
as you are me
and we are all together.

—John Lennon/Paul McCartney
"I Am The Walrus"
1967

Well, not exactly.

After five years of silence, restraint, and privacy, John and Yoko were back on the street, back in the recording studio, planning a tour, and talking with immaculate sanity, care, and optimism about the importance of family, about reversing and coming to terms with masculine-feminine polarities, about the need for hope. And, quietly but firmly, about love and faith in the future. Their buoyancy, candor, and sheer happiness, the obvious thrill they felt in their new album's warm reception and brisk sales, and the feeling that finally the pain was gone, that they were ready to once again get down to (public) work—all this makes the slaying doubly heartbreaking.

> I can't remember anything
> without a sadness
> So deep that it hardly
> becomes known to me.
>
> —John Lennon
> (From a poem in a letter to
> Stu Sutcliffe)
> 1961

For days after Lennon's death, hundreds of people maintained a vigil outside the Dakota apartment building where Lennon lived and was shot, holding candles, singing Beatles songs, or just standing and standing and standing. For some, it was ambulance chasing. For most, it was a show of respect and love and community. Where there is sorrow, Oscar Wilde said, there is holy ground, and the Dakota became a large and sad church.

Around the city where he'd lived, and around the country, people wore black armbands. Pictures of Lennon began appearing in the windows of stores (not simply music stores—hardware stores, dry cleaners, bakeries . . .). Record stores draped their windows in black. Everything was honeycombed with sadness.

In the midst of the sadness, many things that seemed ludicrous and grossly inappropriate. George Martin was continually referred to as the Beatles' manager instead of producer, and in a particularly squalid (if well-intentioned) editorial in the *New York Post,* Clive Barnes wrote that the break-up of the Beatles "was, in effect, the ending of the most famous punk group in history." (What?) Even the dates under his picture

JOHN LENNON
1940/1980

seemed too neat, too precious for someone as unruly and sloppy and anarchic as John Lennon.

2

SEVEN DAYS IN DECEMBER

For nearly twenty years, John Lennon, with indefatigable wit, humor, grace, and candor, defied all efforts to turn his life into one monumental tabloid fact. It took his death by gunfire in one devastating, incomprehensible moment to accomplish that.

"I remember in one interview Lennon was talking about the time he left Yoko," recalls one of his New York fans. "The papers all said Lennon walked out. He was saying it wasn't that simple . . . you never just *walk* anywhere. That's the thing about his death. No matter how often you kick it around in your mind, the fact that John Lennon's dead, it doesn't wash. It's too simple. I'd believe anything about this man except that he's dead . . ."

The sequence of events on Monday, December 8, leading to the dry police memo stating that a man had been "reported shot—victim removed to Roosevelt Hospital" began about 5:00 p.m., when John Lennon and Yoko Ono left their bright, expensive seventh-floor cooperative apartment at the Dakota. Waiting for them outside the 72d Street gates of the giant landmark was a chubby, anxious young man, wearing wire-rimmed glasses and a dark raincoat, and clutching a copy of John and Yoko's *Double Fantasy,* their first LP in five years. The young man had been hanging out near the

Dakota for three days, but it was not deemed unusual for a dedicated fan to make an extended pilgrimage to the Lennon home. This pudgy sad-eyed fan, as the world would learn hours later, was Mark David Chapman.

As the Lennons passed through the wrought-iron front gate and headed for their limo, the fan thrust his album at John, and, as he generally did, Lennon scrawled an autograph across the cover.

Paul Goresh, an amateur photographer who caught a shot of Lennon signing the autograph, struck up a conversation with Chapman. Goresh said he was going home, and that he could get Lennon's autograph another time. Said Chapman, "I'd wait, you never know if you'll see him again."

The Lennons were driven to the Record Plant recording studio on West 44th Street, where they and their producer, Jack Douglas, supervised the mastering of a singles with the tentative title "Walking on Thin Ice," from the *Double Fantasy* LP.

At about 10:30 p.m. saying they were going to get a bite to eat before returning home, John and Yoko left Douglas at the studio, but decided to forgo the meal and headed straight home. At 10:50 p.m., the limo pulled up in front of the 72d Street gates. According to several press accounts, at least three witnesses—a doorman at the entrance, an elevator operator, and a cabbie dropping off a fare—saw Mark Chapman standing silently in the shadow of the building archway. As John and Yoko walked by him, Chapman called out, "Mr. Lennon," quickly pulled a pistol from his coat and dropped into a combat crouch, emptying the .38 caliber Charter Arms short-barreled pistol into Lennon's body. Four shots, two into the back and two into the shoulder, sent Lennon staggering across the entranceway to the door of the concierge's office. "I'm shot," he said, falling face down on the stairs. Yoko ran to his side, screaming, "Help me," as she cradled his head in her arms.

As a half-dozen people scurried about, the doorman

approached Chapman, who had dropped the gun at his side and removed from his coat a copy of J. D. Salinger's *Catcher in the Rye*.

"Do you know what you just did?" the doorman said, kicking the gun away.

"I just shot John Lennon," replied Chapman matter-of-factly. When the first two policemen arrived on the scene moments later, they found Chapman standing in the same spot, reading his book. The elevator man had picked up the gun for safekeeping. Two more policemen arrived. One of them, Officer James Moran, lifted Lennon into the back seat of the patrol car. Lennon was moaning softly. "Are you John Lennon?" asked the officer. "Yeah," the wounded man gurgled. The car speeded to Roosevelt Hospital on 59th Street and Ninth Avenue, where the 40-year-old ex-Beatle was pronounced dead on arrival at 11:15.

"It wasn't possible to resuscitate him by any means," said Dr. Stephen Lynn, the hospital's director of emergency services. "He'd lost three to four quarts of blood, about 80 percent of his blood volume." It was Lynn who informed Yoko of her husband's death, after the surgeons had given up after a half hour of effort.

"Where's my husband?" Yoko asked him. "I want to be with my husband. He would want me to be with him." Lynn said, "We have very bad news. Unfortunately, in spite of massive efforts, your husband is dead. There was no suffering at the end." "Are you saying he's sleeping?" sobbed Yoko, refusing to accept the statement at face value.

While the doctors worked, the paparazzi and newsmen arrived, as did a few fans. One reporter tried to march through the doors with a film crew, but was stopped. Accompanied by David Geffen, whose record company had released the Lennons' new LP, Yoko left the hospital, returning home about midnight. She placed three telephone calls—to Julian, John's son by his previous marriage; to John's aunt, Mimi Smith, who had raised him; and to Paul McCartney.

Back at Roosevelt Hospital, Dr. Lynn was giving a

hastily assembled press conference, fielding a barrage of questions. Patiently, he described the location of the wounds to the point where it meant nothing. The crowd at the hospital was soon composed mainly of fans, as newsmen left to file their stories or to cover the scene at the Dakota.

"I'm going to kneel here all night by the base of the wall and pray for the soul of John Lennon," said a dark-haired man in a rumpled sports jacket, standing near the emergency entrance. "I invite all of you to join. John Lennon's spirit was our spirit." Another arrival told of being at a nearby rock club, Hurrah's, when word of the shooting spread like smoke across the dance floor. "Everybody was stunned. The place just emptied right out. Some went up to 72d Street, some came down here."

Ellie Greenwich, who wrote "Be My Baby," a song Lennon had recorded five years earlier, was a bystander at the hospital. "What he gave the world can't be comprehended," she said. Others were in various states of shock, unable to talk or find adequate words.

By 1:00 a.m., a crowd of a thousand had gathered at the Dakota. The police found it necessary to cordon off 72d Street from Central Park West to Columbus Avenue. In a scene that was being repeated in several large cities across America, the people circled the block chanting, singing, praying, wailing, and simply remembering.

"It's the end of an era," said one well-dressed man in his thirties. The Dakota, everyone seemed to agree, would remain a shrine from this day forth. By the next afternoon, the filigreed gate was covered with flowers, photos, and other memorial memorabilia. Yoko Ono issued two messages in the hours after the shooting. The first statement was: "John loved and prayed for the human race. Please do the same for him." Later, a message came down that the noise was disturbing. "Doesn't she understand," cried a teenage fan, "that we're here because we love John and Yoko?"

As the specter of John Lennon's death proved too much for many to accept, thoughts turned to Mark

David Chapman, who within two hours of the killing had become an entry in America's assassination lexicon. Perhaps the history of bloodshed was condemned to repeat itself, but the police had learned their lesson from Dallas. Mark Chapman was placed under an airtight security lid, hustled from place to place in CIA-type secrecy, attired in a bulletproof vest. In a matter of days, we would know almost everything about Chapman—except his motive for killing John Lennon.

According to Texas records, Mark Chapman was born in Fort Worth on May 10, 1955, to David Curtis Chapman and Diane Elizabeth Pease Chapman. The father was serving at a local air force base. The family moved to Atlanta when Mark was a boy. His father, who currently lives in a white frame-and-brick house in northeastern Atlanta, spoke of his son as an "industrious, cheerful, likable" teenager. After watching Mark's life unfold in bits and pieces on the television news, the senior Mr. Chapman sighed, "It's just like a different person than I used to know."

A retired oil company executive now employed by a local bank, forty-nine-year-old David Chapman, who was a strict disciplinarian as a father, went on to speak of his son's love of the Beatles, noting that he had taught his son to play box guitar when the boy was only seven. He said he had not seen Mark since 1977 and decided it was best not to come to visit his son in a New York jail.

"I remember him only as a quiet, low-key face in the crowd," wrote Kellie Cannon in the *Dallas Morning News* of December 10. Cannon, a classmate of Chapman's at Columbia High School in Decatur, Georgia, had, like almost all Chapman's classmates and friends from that period, lost contact with him.

Cannon, in quoting other high-school acquaintances of Chapman's, offered up a litany all-too-familiar to those who grew up in the last two decades.

"He was just a real quiet, normal guy," said one Columbia H.S. alumna. Yet another recalled Chapman's graduation photo in the *Aquila,* the school's yearbook, which portrayed a brown-haired, blue-eyed neophyte with hair combed low on his forehead, Beatles-style.

Not surprisingly, however, most of his classmates could remember few specifics about Chapman's activities in Decatur. If he stands out at all in any of their minds, it is for the things he didn't do. For example, he was cited as the only senior in the school band who was not elected a band captain by his peers.

Cheryl Cater, identified by Kellie Cannon as one of Chapman's closest high-school friends, points to Chapman's major distinguishing feature—an obsession with the music, personalities, and total aura of the Beatles. Twenty-five-year-old Mark David Chapman was only eight years old when the Beatles broke internationally, yet in the afterglow, they burned more strongly for him than for most of those old enough to have experienced their coming in its full force.

Friends said Chapman's room was a shrine to the Fab Four, with the walls full of photos and press clips, and a record cabinet dominated by Beatle LPs and the later Beatle solo projects. Classmates remember that Chapman's English assignments were invariably half-baked treatises on the group. Friends say that as an amateur guitarist, Chapman aped Lennon's style.

Friends also say he experimented with LSD and ran away from home at fourteen to hole up with a classmate. The second time he ran away he went to Los Angeles—or so he told his buddies.

One curious note from his high-school period—classmates say that around the tenth or eleventh grade, he turned into a "Jesus freak," shortening his hair and neatening up his dress. One old friend of Chapman's recalls attending a revival meeting with him at which "people began speaking in tongues."

Chapman complained of not "finding anyone who would listen to me." Pressed about his own emotional afflictions, Chapman would turn the conversation toward his favorite subject: the Beatles and the depth of their lyrical message. "He was always talking about just getting away from everything," says a close friend.

If we accept the psychological dictum that murder is a variation on suicide, then in killing John Lennon, young Chapman fulfilled his aim at last.

After graduation, Chapman drifted into DeKalb Community College and dropped out quickly. Though he was said to harbor dreams of a rock-and-roll career, his true calling was children. "He was a regular Pied Piper," says Vince Smith, who counseled Chapman at the YMCA in Decatur. Chapman worked for a brief time as a YMCA camp counselor, without much enthusiasm, but friends said he perked up noticeably when informed of a job in Beirut, Lebanon, opening up a youth hostel. In June 1975, he left for Lebanon, but the civil war forced him back to the States in two weeks. He was said to be bitterly disappointed. However, David Moore, a YMCA official who met Mark after his return from Beirut, recalled a tape recording Chapman had made of machine-gun fire. Moore said that Chapman had found his two weeks in Lebanon "exciting" and would occasionally play the tape for others.

Chapman's association with the YMCA continued when he went to work at a camp for Vietnamese refugees run by Moore at Fort Chaffee, Arkansas. Chapman naturally gravitated toward the Vietnamese children. "He was one of the most compassionate, sensitive young people I've ever met," said Moore, pointing to a side of Chapman not hitherto recognized by his peers.

Chapman worked at the resettlement camp for about six months, or until Fort Chaffee stopped admitting refugees. Around this time, say those close to Chapman, he began an affair with a woman named Jessica. "He was madly in love with her and she kind of straightened him around," says Moore, referring to the fact that two years after leaving Atlanta, Chapman remained troubled by questions of identity and had yet to forswear drugs.

At the reported urging of Jessica, Chapman enrolled at Covenant College, a tiny Reform Presbyterian school in Tennessee, but, as in an earlier college stint, he did not have the discipline and flunked out after one semester. Said Moore, "He became unglued when he couldn't cut it in school and the girl told him to pack off."

Which is what Chapman eventually did, heading for Hawaii—but first, he took a security guard training course in Atlanta, scoring 88 on a pistol firing test (the passing grade was 60). He worked for a while as a guard in Atlanta, finally leaving for Hawaii in early 1977. However, he could not shake the aftereffects of his failed romance. In August of that year, he began working in the print shop of Castle Memorial Hospital on the island of Oahu. Paul Tharp, the hospital's PR director, said Chapman was not only a good worker, but "made a lot of friends" and showed no evidence of antisocial tendencies, at least on the job.

Nevertheless, Chapman is reported to have made the first of two botched suicide attempts in Honolulu in 1977—the second was in New York two weeks before the Lennon shooting—running a tube from the exhaust through his car window. He was institutionalized for a short time at Castle, but his negative attitude had not changed by the following year when he visited David Moore at the YMCA's World Alliance conference in Geneva. He spoke of his constant pining for Jessica and his nervous breakdown, plus the breakup of his parents' marriage, which occurred in early 1978 after the Chapmans returned from a visit with their son in Hawaii. The divorce apparently unsettled Mark as much as the unhappy affair. "He was devastated by it," says Moore. "He loved them both so much . . ."

When Chapman returned from an around-the-world sojourn, he renewed his acquaintance with the woman who had booked the tour. In June 1979, Gloria Abe and Chapman were married and settled in downtown Honolulu. Gloria, a diminutive woman of Japanese ancestry who was four years mark's senior, continued to work at the travel agency. Meanwhile, Mark's mother had relocated to Hawaii to start life anew as a divorcee.

Friends say it didn't take long for cracks to appear

in the relationship of Mark and Gloria. It was said that at their first meeting, Gloria had been "flattered" by the attention Chapman had paid to her since "she liked Caucasians but had no suitors." However, Chapman eventually began making unreasonable demands, forcing Gloria to quit her job. Friends also said Chapman was harsh with his wife. "Gloria felt she could help him," said a friend. "She was beautiful," added a co-worker at the travel agency, "But he [Chapman] was a creep . . . he hated everything good in the world. He was like a 'Blue Meanie.' "

Gloria Chapman, who initially went into seclusion after the shooting, later said in an interview that she still loved her husband and "as a Christian, I believe forgiveness is a very important thing. I have always been a forgiving person, and I always forgave Mark when he did things in the past."

About a year ago, Mark Chapman left his job at the hospital for a position as a security guard at a condominium project. Though he only earned about $4 an hour, Chapman spent thousands of dollars for artworks and antiques.

His major interest was in surrealism, and he bought a copy of a Salvador Dali print which showed the assassinated President Lincoln, later selling it to buy something less harrowing, a $7500 Norman Rockwell lithograph, "Triple Self-Portrait."

Gloria and Mark lived in a $425-a-month one-bedroom condominium apartment in the Diamond Head Tower at Kukui Plaza. Chapman's mother is believed to have lent her son several thousand dollars for his trips to New York, and he borrowed $2500 from the Castle Hospital credit union.

According to Honolulu police, Chapman applied for, and received, a pistol permit in October. On October 27 he purchased the Charter Arms pistol at J&S Enterprises—Guns, Honolulu, for $169. The pistol is of a kind that is easily concealed. Police said they had no reason to deny Chapman the permit, as he had no criminal record.

Chapman's last day as an unarmed security guard in

a Honolulu condominium complex was October 23. That evening, he signed himself out as "John Lennon." His bosses discovered it the following morning when they checked the log, but probably thought it nothing more than a bizarre gag.

In early November, Chapman left Hawaii for Atlanta, where he visited several old acquaintances, but not his father, as he had said he would. Madison Short, his high-school chorus teacher, said Chapman insisted he was "happy," but others he visited said he seemed depressed. Chapman's next reported stop was New York, where he stayed for a short time before heading back to Hawaii.

On December 5, he left Hawaii to return to New York, arriving on December 6.

Police have zeroed in on the last three days before the shooting. On Saturday, shortly before noon, Chapman registered under his own name at the YMCA on 63d Street, near Central Park West, nine blocks from the Dakota. The following day, he registered at the Sheraton Centre Hotel at 52d Street and 7th Avenue, about a mile from the Dakota, again using his real name and Hawaii address. Sunday night he charged a $15 dinner to his room.

A cabdriver, who says he picked up Chapman at 8th Avenue and 55th Street on Saturday night, describes Chapman as talking excitedly about "dropping off the tapes of an album John Lennon and Paul McCartney made today . . . I was the engineer and they played for three hours straight." "He seemed like a real John Lennon fan," cabbie Mark Snyder told the *New York Post*. "He knew a lot of details about him and the music business." Snyder said he took Chapman on a crazy-quilt ride across town, making stops along the way on the upper West Side, upper East Side, and the Village. Chapman, Snyder said, seemed "agitated."

Chapman was seen loitering near the Dakota on Saturday, Sunday, and Monday. A construction worker at the building who left work at 8:30 p.m. Monday— 2-1/2 hours before the shooting—spotted Chapman in conversation with the guard at the front gate. The worker said he remembered seeing Chapman around the building all weekend. "He stood out from all the other autograph seekers because he was fatter." This three-day period, said legal sources, will be the crucial factor in the case, as Chapman will probably plead not guilty by reason of insanity, and the prosecution will seek to prove criminal intent.

Several days after the shooting, startling new evidence suggested that Chapman's Lennon fixation might have taken an evil form as far back as 1975. A BBC film of a Lennon concert in England is said to show Chapman sitting near the stage and "glaring" at the performer.

The day after the fatal shooting, Mark Chapman was arraigned in Manhattan Criminal Court on charges of second-degree murder and possession of a revolver. His attorney suggested that Chapman was "not fully cognizant of what is going on in these proceedings," while police officials said Chapman had made a confession and alluded to "hearing voices" and having been forced into the act by "the devil."

In any case, whether it turns out that Lennon had been a marked man for years, or simply the victim of one moment of flashing insanity, the lives of killer and victim were doubtless intertwined through a full generation. Perhaps the most hideous aspect of the crime was the realization that, in this respect, Mark David Chapman was one of us—a fan, an admirer, a young man who charted his life along a map of Beatle music and lyrics.

Psychiatric theories about Chapman's sudden aberrant behavior abound. The most harrowing of these, described by one expert as "superidentification," seems to make the most sense. From childhood in which his parents forbade the playing of Beatles records, he grew to manhood identifying with John Lennon, the "most rebellious" member of the group. As his sense of self-esteem and personal identity faded like the image on a badly developed photograph, he gradually took on the image of his "hero" John Lennon.

Following this logic, Chapman's secret obsession may possibly have continued as a private fantasy forever, as long as Lennon remained in retirement. Lennon's emergence from five years self-exile may have triggered Chapman's realization that his "secret life" of "being John Lennon" would have to end. Lennon was back in the public eye. Chapman could not "be" there, too.

Obsession changed to the worst kind of hatred: self-hatred. It had become as intolerable for him not to "be" John Lennon as it was for him to remain Mark David Chapman. By killing his self idol, he may have been trying to exorcise his fantasy self and by destroying that, destroy himself.

Perhaps, in the star-crossed relationship of Chapman and John Lennon, we saw a dark side of ourselves. Despite the fact that, of all the Beatles, John Lennon was the one whom you felt you might have known as a friend, co-worker, or lovable eccentric neighbor, he was saddled with celebrityhood and could never fully get it off his back. As a celebrity, Lennon had the power to make an identity for himself in the world. That fame offered to others a promise of self-realization—a promise that no artist can deliver on. The music of the Beatles, and the hopes and goodwill it symbolized, couldn't help Mark Chapman make sense of his life, or make him be what he needed to be. Unlike the other hopeless people, he took the easy way out.

Chapman was first taken to Bellevue Hospital and placed on an around-the-clock "suicide watch," but fears of a revenge killing or of a crowd demonstration spilling over to the hospital led police to transfer Chapman to the more remote Riker's Island jail for thirty days of psychiatric tests.

Meanwhile, several curious events were reported in the aftermath of the Lennon slaying. Chapman's first court-appointed attorney, Herbert Adlerberg, resigned from the case. "What's happened in the last few days has been beyond any proportion I believed it would be," said the sixty-year-old attorney, who has handled a number of highly controversial cases in the past, including that of the Black Liberation Army members accused of killing New York City policemen. Though denying receipt of death threats, the lawyer said the notoriety of the case had resulted in his spending most of his time fielding phone calls. "It would be detrimental to the defendant if I stayed on the case," he concluded.

Attorney Jonathan Marks, a much younger man at thirty-seven, accepted the case. Marks made it plain that he was a long-time Beatles fan, but that every citizen deserves a defense. "Chapman," he said, giving his initial impressions of his client, "appears to be a man desperately in need of a friend, and was grateful for someone at his side when the rest of the world was against him."

In another development, the medical examiner's office began an investigation into the circumstances surrounding the publication of a front-page *New York Post* photo of John Lennon's body at the city morgue. The *Post* was the subject of a similar investigation several years ago when it published a photo of "Son of Sam" killer David Berkowitz asleep in his jail cell.

Finally, Chapman, after reading a scrawled death threat on a prison wall at Riker's, believed fellow inmates might try to poison him and went on a two-day fast. The ex-security guard, whose possessions upon his arrest consisted of 14 hours of Beatles tapes, the Bible, the Salinger book, $2000, and a gun, broke his fast with dinner on December 14.

The day after the shooting, Yoko Ono remained secluded in her Dakota apartment, sending a friend downstairs to receive messages, poems, and garlands of flowers sent by friends and admirers. With her were a number of close friends, including Ringo Starr and his fiancée Barbara Bach, who flew in from Europe, and

David Geffen. Elliot Mintz, a Los Angeles publicist and friend of the Lennons, said the mood was "just grim" in the Lennon apartment, adding that despite the urging of friends, Yoko had refused to see a doctor. "She is determined to find the strength to write a statement to the world which she hopes can adequately reflect her thoughts and what John would have wanted to say."

What followed the next day was not a major statement, but something very close to the heart—a letter written on family stationery, relating that Yoko had told her five-year-old son, Sean, about his father's death:

> I told Sean what happened. I showed him the picture of his father on the cover of the paper and explained the situation. I took Sean to the spot where John lay after he was shot. Sean wanted to know why the person shot John if he liked John. I explained that he was probably a confused person. Sean said we should find out if he was confused or if he really had meant to kill John. I said that was up to the court. He asked what court—a tennis court or a basketball court? That's how Sean used to talk with his father. They were buddies. John would have been proud of Sean if he had heard this. Sean cried later. He also said "Now daddy is part of God. I guess when you die you become much more bigger because you're part of everything."
>
> I don't have much more to add to Sean's statement. The silent vigil will take place December 14th at 2 p.m. for ten minutes.
>
> Our thoughts will be with you.
>
> Love, Yoko & Sean.

John Lennon's body was taken to a crematory in Westchester County. No funeral services were held, and the ashes were interred privately in England. Lennon had, in interviews, expressed his distaste for the carnival atmosphere surrounding the death of Elvis Presley.

Yoko took pains to deflect the heat from New York City, her and John's home for nine years. "People say there's something wrong with New York," she told *Los Angeles Times* writer Robert Hilburn, "but John loved New York. He'd be the first to say it wasn't New York's fault. There can be one crank anywhere." Yoko sat in her dimly lit bedrooom and described the scene at the shooting: "We were walking to the entrance of the building when I heard the shot . . . I didn't realize at first that John had been hit. He kept walking. Then he fell and I saw the blood . . ." Yoko fought back tears as she told of the couple's plans to "live until we were eighty. We even drew up lists of all the things we could do together for all those years. Then, it was all over . . . But that doesn't mean the message should be over. The music will live on."

Though Yoko had called for ten minutes of silent prayer for her late husband, the thoughts of millions were focused on John Lennon throughout the week. The reaction from around the world was of a magnitude not seen since the Kennedy assassination of the sixties. Perhaps the pointlessness of the death increased the intensity of its effect.

From Paul, George, and Ringo came condolences. George called the shooting an "outrage," asking rhetorically how it was that a man with so much to give and such a strong sense of self could be slain by someone with virtually no self at all. Paul McCartney, appearing on national television here, seemed to many almost flippant in calling the Lennon killing a "drag," but others suspected that the death of Lennon—the big brother who had turned him away—had left McCartney too devastated to risk betrayal of his true feelings.

In Europe, John's ex-wife Cynthia, whose book had taken some caustic shots at John, and Ringo's ex-wife Maureen mourned together, while Julian Lennon—who is the image of what his father looked like twenty years ago—came to New York to help Yoko mourn.

Show-biz friends and Dakota neighbors expressed

shock and bewilderment. George Martin, the Beatles' producer, described his reaction as "stunned beyond belief." Sid Bernstein, the promoter who introduced the Beatles to America sixteen years ago and who has been promoting a reunion ever since, said he hoped the other three members would get together "and make some sort of memorial to John."

The politicos weighed in with their condolences. Most predictable was the President-elect of the United States, who deplored the killing as a "great tragedy," and added that "we have to find an answer to street violence" without mentioning control of the flood of handguns. President Carter said, "Lennon's spirit, the spirit of the Beatles—brash and earnest, ironic and idealistic all at once—became the spirit of a whole generation . . . he leaves an extraordinary and permanent legacy . . . I am saddened by his death and distressed by the senseless manner of it. It is especially poignant that John Lennon has died by violence, though he had long campaigned for peace."

New York Mayor Edward Koch elected to sponsor the Central Park vigil on December 14, on behalf of the city.

From around the world came reports of all-night singalongs, prayer meetings, candle-lighting ceremonies, and other forms of tribute.

For certain mourners across America, life without John Lennon was unbearable. Sixteen-year-old Colleen Costello overdosed on sleeping pills and died, leaving a brief note that she was depressed because of "the killing of John Lennon up in New York." Michael Craig, a thirty-year-old unemployed Salt Lake City man, shot himself in the head. Lisa Renak, a neighbor, said they were sharing a bowl of granola when she asked his feelings about the Lennon death. "I think I'll end the whole damn thing," she quoted Craig as saying before he pulled a .25 caliber pistol from his pocket and fired it into his mouth.

On the Brava coast of Spain, an aging Salvador Dali learned of Lennon's death from a local newspaper. "He was a good man, a close friend," said Dali, horrified that the killer had mounted Dali's Lincoln painting as his living-room showpiece.

Reaction was strongest in America, not only in terms of mourning vigils, but in dollars and cents. Thousands of record shops reported runs on Beatle LPs and Lennon solo albums. "I think people realize that these aren't limited edition items and there'll be plenty of time to buy them next week," said one store clerk. "But people have a need to have something of John Lennon's *right now*. To be able to feel a part of his life and closer to the spirit of mourning . . ."

In New York—the focus of activity in the week after the shooting—radio stations scrapped play lists, television stations broadcast Beatles retrospectives, and the Dakota vigil continued around the clock, much to the consternation of some of its celebrity tenants, who were anxious to resume their own lives and put the fear and shock of the Lennon assassination behind them.

Midwest college campuses held vigils and memorial concerts while radio stations played non-stop Beatles and listeners stormed record outlets. Three hundred Indiana University students formed a large circle and offered a public prayer, while Southern Illinois University students marched in a candlelight procession Tuesday night, following a memorial service.

In Houston, Texas, many people remembered John and Yoko's visit in 1971. The couple had come in quest of Yoko's daughter, who was being held by her ex-husband, the nomadic documentary filmmaker Anthony Cox. Though they eventually won custody of the eight-year-old Kyoto, the child was spirited away, never to be seen again.

In Philadelphia, Bruce Springsteen opened his Tuesday night show with a tribute: "It's a hard night to come out and play when so much has been lost," Springsteen said. "The first song I ever learned was a record called "Twist and Shout" and if it wasn't for John Lennon, we'd all be in a different place tonight." The crowd erupted in bittersweet agreement.

In Los Angeles, one thousand John Lennon fans

gathered underneath a thirty-five-foot Christmas tree in the ABC Complex. A memorial service was held. Some cried, a handful cursed Mark Chapman, but most simply held candles above their heads and sang, "All we are saying, is give peace a chance." It was not an entirely mournful scene. Incense and marijuana were in abundance. At one point during the proceedings, the MC, a local disk jockey, held up a headline announcement, "THE DREAM IS OVER."

"It's not over!" hollered another DJ.

In other parts of the world, large masses of people demonstrated their grief and anger, most notably in John's native city of Liverpool, England. In the week after his death, the bleak factory town experienced its first economic mini-boom in years as record and memorabilia shops were briskly moving goods. "I've always listened to me friend's albums before," said a Liverpudlian in her thirties, "but now I want my own." At the Magical Mystery Store, a customer said proudly that the town that John Lennon had left in life had reclaimed him in death.

The city council issued a statement of "shock and dismay" that was "More keenly felt in Liverpool—his home city." Sometime in January, a memorial service was to be held at the Liverpool Cathedral, the city's biggest Anglican church. The city's mayor, who has been trying for years to raise money for a permanent Beatles tribute, thought that now the depressed burg might at last find a way to make that dream come true.

Enterprising citizens have already created a monument in Liverpool. Near the site of the Cavern Club where the Beatles played their first gigs (now a parking lot) and next door to Brady's, an existing punk club, a boarded-up doorway is adorned with a small madonna, holding the four Beatles in her arms. Under the shrine are a bevy of cards and flowers. One unsigned card reads, "Dear John, now at last you've found your peace."

The English media used Lennon's demise to mourn the passing of a better time. Noted the *Times* of

London, "England truly emerged from its postwar depression and became a nation of joyful and envied achievement [in the sixties] ... [Lennon's death], untimely and inappropriately violent, commits to history the decade that so utterly changed British history." With classic British propriety, pride, and prejudice, the *Times* went on to blame America. "That couldn't happen here," said a Londoner, "people just don't have guns." America's loose gun control laws took a pounding in the *New Standard,* which railed that the killing "was increasingly typical of New York and the U.S. in general, where the freedom to carry guns brought forth monsters."

Strong reactions to the murder were felt in Germany—Bavarian Radio veered from its usual beer garden music to play "Ballad of John and Yoko"—and in Austria, where national TV devoted peak-time programming to a tribute to Lennon.

Behind the Iron Curtain, where Lennon and the Beatles had been branded prime examples of capitalist decadence, the reaction was guarded sadness. Moscow radio played an hour and a half of old Beatles and Lennon solo tunes the Tuesday evening following his death. The state media called the late musician a leader in the struggle for world peace and in the anti-Vietnam War movement. The Soviets also used Lennon's death to blast the "dirty initiatives of the U.S. military." Lennon had opposed them, said the Soviets, as a result had nearly been prevented from living in America.

The death of John Lennon also served as yet another in an all-too-long string of rallying points for the nation's gun control advocates. From those on the other side of the politico/social spectrum, his death stirred cries for stricter sentencing, and a return to the death penalty on a major scale.

Lennon's death was also mourned by the intelligentsia, which had belatedly recognized him as one of them. John Leonard, writing in the *New York Times* of December 14, noted that "we listened [to the Beatles], instead of merely throbbing." He attributed this to Lennon's influence, for "he read Joyce, whereas Mick Jagger reads comic books and—I'm sorry to say—Bob Dylan and Bruce Springsteen read Khalil Gibran and Hermann Hesse." Added Leonard, "We got the rage, the sorrow, the yearning, the vulnerability, plus the laugh-track, an ironic scourge."

In the masses of newsprint, one was able to find only a few mentions of Lennon's frailties: his bouts with ego, his irresponsible bestowal of an imprimatur on the use of lysergic acid, his sometimes rampant foolishness—but in his death, as in life, he was readily forgiven. As much as his return to recording music was applauded, his devotion to family and his disinclination to follow fashion were accorded great respect.

On Sunday, December 14 at 2:00 p.m., the world-wide mourning reached its climax, or maybe the first of a series of climaxes, as dozens of radio stations broadcast memorials or went off the air for ten minutes of silent prayer. At Shea Stadium in New York where the New York Jets were playing the New Orleans Saints in a National Football League contest of also-rans, half-time ceremonies featured a John Lennon tribute. Large crowds turned out in every major American city. An outdoor memorial concert in Liverpool drew tens of thousands.

Yet nothing compared with the scene in New York's Central Park bandshell where 100,000 stood in stone silence for ten minutes, the only sound a small voice asking, "Why is everybody so quiet?" Facing a lone poster of John Lennon in his New York City t-shirt, this crowd was, in a sense, not a crowd at all but 100,000 individuals wrapped up in their own reveries. Some had signs—JOHN LIVES—GIVE PEACE A CHANCE —most had only their memories and a need to express their grief in the proper form.

Later, as the recorded Lennon music faded and the crowd drifted toward the Dakota to continue the vigil, Yoko was indeed watching. Her message to the thousands below her window came in verse form: "I saw

John smiling in the sky...I saw all of us becoming one mind." All those private thoughts, hopes, and disillusionments had become public.

As of this writing, the mourning period seems far from over. The death of John Lennon, so abrupt and senseless, has generated no cathartic relief. So the vigil goes on. Eventually, Lennon's legacy will rest in his music, his family, and the millions of musicians and listeners he influenced. His memory will also remain somehow embedded in the streets of the upper East and West Sides and Greenwich Village areas in which he lived and worked. For New York had become his home in every way a man can have a home. Paraphrasing Robert Frost, New York did not have to take John Lennon in—it took him in because he deserved it.

His impact upon the city was both great and small: as great as the weight of 8 million fans and the government that fought to keep him from them; as small as the 72d Street candy store with the infantile crayon-lettered sign in the window, "We'll miss you, John."

3

SOMETIME IN N.Y.C.

John Lennon and Yoko Ono became residents of New York City in August 1971, though the city's magnetic force had been exerting its pull on them for years.

It was December 1970, and John and Yoko are making avant-garde films in a seventh-floor soundstage on West 61st Street. The film is called *Up Your Legs Forever,* and in reality, it is not John and Yoko's film at all, since they have no U.S. work permits and are forced to sit behind a screen and watch a parade of volunteers stand on the podium while a camera pans up their bare legs from toes to hips. Among those "donating their legs for peace" are actor George Segal, *Rolling Stone* publisher Jann Wenner, artist Larry Rivers, and moviemaker D. A. Pennebaker. Writer Al Aronowitz, a reluctant number 284 on the cast list, disrobes to his underwear, all the while remembering John Lennon's immortal words when the Beatles landed on our shores for the first time: "A little lunacy is good for the soul." "Haven't you seen enough of these?" says Aronowitz, motioning toward his lower body. "No," says Lennon, "but I'm getting cured." "What will you do next?" asks Aronowitz. "I dunno," says the budding filmmaker. "There must be something else."

"Well, if I couldn't get free [of the Beatles]," John

Lennon is saying," who else the hell could? As we used
to say, we [the Beatles] were the center of the storm,
we were the eye—we were the calm in the middle—
everybody else was crazy, not us. Just sitting in rooms
talking about it, thinking up the next game . . ."

In mid-1971, John Lennon and Yoko Ono move
directly into the center of the storm, high above Manhattan on the seventeenth floor of the St. Regis Hotel.
Their room is cluttered with film-editing equipment,
stereo equipment, stacks of Chuck Berry albums, and
books by noted leftists Dan Berrigan and Paul Krass-
ner. John has obtained a six-month, nonrenewable
visa, but his 1968 conviction in England for possession
of marijuana is looming larger in their future. The
press slagging, which is to continue on and off for four
years, has begun. "It's absolutely disgusting," snaps
Lennon of one particularly bitter piece of journalism.
Yoko seems depressed and John is doing everything
possible to kiss and fondle the depression away. Lennon seems gentler, sweeter than his image as a biting
cynic. "We're looking around for an apartment," he
tells the *Washington Post*. "I didn't like New York at
first but now I've come to love it. It's dead in London
compared to living here. London's still a nice place to
go for a rest, but this is where everything is happening."

Lennon on Dick Cavett's show in September 1971:
"It could have been great fun [the Beatles], but not
forever." In England the next day, George Harrison
mentions the possibility of a Beatles reunion before
Christmas. The seventies are going to be a long and
winding road for all of us.

In 1971, the Lennons humbly jump into the breach
of the Greenwich Village rock scene, and once again,
John Lennon is accused of fomenting sexual upheaval
among the young. A Bible Belt crusader warns of "sex
in the streets" by 1974. Inspiring his diatribe is the
telecast image of John and Yoko on their bed in the
village, Yoko beating a tom-tom, John pluckiing away
at his steel soundbox, as Jerry Rubin, John Sinclair,

and the cream of the yipster movement sit around in wonder.

David Peel, "the musical mayor" of New York, meets John and Yoko on St. Marks Place, and they agree to come hear Peel give a street concert. "No normal people ever come to see me play," says Peel, who sings "Hava Marijuana" and "The Pope Smokes Dope," which delight the Lennons. Peel calls them "completely synchronized, talking to one's like talking to both." The group marches through the streets singing and David Peel goes home and writes a song about it: "You played and jammed at Fillmore East/You shopped on New York streets/You also met an underground/ Welcome to a freaky town."

The scene gets even freakier. David Peel is signed to Apple Records and John and Yoko are spending a lot of time in bed; in fact they do most of their business there, including TV interviews. One day they invite Jerry Rubin to join them in the sack. "You should be a member of the band," John tells Rubin. "If you're gonna work with us [politically], you should play music with us."

John and Yoko immerse themselves in what was then a fledgling "underground" music scene in New York, as John practices with Elephant's Memory and hangs out at Max's Kansas City, which is beginning to pass through the era of loud noise. The Lennons host the Mike Douglas show for one zany week, and jam with the teacher, Chuck Berry.

The nation's leading radical thinkers seem to accept John and Yoko as fellow travelers and potential saviors. The results of his primal scream therapy find their way into Lennon's music, in the sheer force of his lyrics. Andrew Kopkind, writing in *Ramparts*, suggests that Lennon's music represents the necessity of "freeing ourselves from the isolation of private existence in a mass audience." The myths of Hare Krishna and log cabins in Vermont are not what it is about. John Lennon in his first months in New York, in the very beginning of his long struggle to be free of the

Beatles, is, at least to the still functioning left, a living
symbol of anti-isolationist solidarity and mass liberation.

By 1972, the Lennons, having been refused permanent residence in the U.S., but comfortably ensconced
in a two-bedroom duplex in the West Village, are
being compared with Scott and Zelda Fitzgerald: to
wit, a creative, tortured couple, carrying around the
ghosts that will eventually break them apart. They
have been in New York for only sixteen months, but
are already city institutions—shopworn and irrepressible, like Greenwich Village. And like institutions, they are learning that in the center of the storm,
in the media capital of the world, it is possible to blend
right in with the surroundings in a most satisfying way.
Many years later, just two days before his death, in an
interview with BBC disk jockey Andy Peebles, Lennon
will talk about that feeling: "In early years I would be
walking all tense, waiting for somebody to say something or jump on me and like that . . . and it took me
two years to unwind. I can go right out of this door
now and go into a restaurant. Do you know how great
that is? They just say 'Oh hey, how ya doin', like your
record' . . ." By '72, John Lennon's love affair with
New York has begun in earnest.

Later that year, the Lennons appear tired. It has
been a busy twelve months: TV appearances, a "One-
to-One" benefit in Central Park in August to benefit
the retarded, two smash shows at Madison Square
Garden for the same purpose, film screenings to decid-
edly mixed reviews, and more bad press—now cen-
tered on their marriage. Says Yoko, "People look
forward to it [our divorce] the way they did our marriage." In addition, the Lennons have just released
"Woman Is the Nigger of the World," which most
radio stations won't play because of the adverse public
reaction. Says Lennon, "The fact that it causes such
excitement is an event in itself. It's like Zen—you can't
unknow what you know . . ."

On top of all this, the past eight months have been
lived beneath the dangling sword of deportation. "All
we can do is wait," sighs Lennon of the machination of

the U.S. Immigration and Naturalization Service. John parries most of the questions about himself, deflecting them toward Yoko and her work. Both of them seem restless and confused in interviews. "It's very bad," says Lennon. "The worst part is we can't leave and we're people used to traveling." (Yoko has custody of her daughter on condition that she remain in America, although the child is in hiding with her natural father.) Meanwhile, in the media swirl of music, marriage, family, legal and world affairs, John Lennon is showing leanings of a different kind, presaging the househusband he will become in the mid-1970s. He speaks of a recent visit to the Nevada desert, during which "We got out and wrote our names big in the sand. We were just two people!"

Through it all, Lennon finds increasing support in many quarters. Pete Hamill in the *New York Post:* "Lennon loves New York ... What an extraordinary thing: a man who changed modern music and profoundly changed modern lifestyles wants to live in New York at the same time that others are going on the lam ... just knowing that John Lennon is in town must change the way we feel about New York. He has improved this town just by showing up."

Whether or not the general populace believes John and Yoko are involved in anything more than good-natured artistic horseplay, the government presses on in its efforts to rid our shores of their influence. In March 1973, Lennon is given 60 days to leave the country by a U.S. immigration judge, while Yoko is declared a permanent resident. (Years later, it will be said the government really wanted Yoko out, but thought the best way to get at her was through John.) The reason for the judge's ruling: John's 1968 British marijuana conviction. Two weeks later, Lennon announces his appeal, noting that "a lot of cases may hinge on this one." He tells a news conference, "America is a place to be in, rather than just scootin' in and out with the loot." His arm around Yoko, he says, "We'll always be together." Character witnesses for John Lennon include New York Mayor John Lindsay,

Dick Cavett, United Auto Workers president Leonard Woodcock, and Jerry Rubin, Abbie Hoffman, and the rest of the old crew seem part of another century. Meanwhile, the man who as New York mayor will sponsor John Lennon's largest memorial, Ed Koch, introduces a bill in Congress to allow the attorney general to admit Lennon to residency.

In October 1973, John Lennon files suit in Manhattan federal court seeking government records on his deportation proceeding, and asking that the immigration board's decision be rejected.

The following month, Lennon is back before a meeting of the Immigration Service's appeals board, asking that he be allowed to stay in America pending a ruling on the lawsuits. Conceivably, sighs the chairman of the appeals panel, this could take years.

In March 1974, John Lennon has been in the U.S. for a year, despite being ordered to leave, and his flustered attorney reports that his marriage is an "on again off again" proposition. During the separation from Yoko, John lives in Hollywood where, according to all press accounts, he creates havoc. While being bounced from L.A.'s Troubador nightclub with his secretary, Mary Pang, Lennon throws a right at a woman photographer, who files a complaint. Police respond to a report of wild female screams at Lennon's bachelor pad, and find Lennon and a female companion, in the words of *Time* magazine, "enjoying a Mr. and Mrs."

In January 1974, Lennon tells the *Los Angeles Times* that the Fab Four might "possibly" reunite, a remark that surely shows his state of confusion.

Lennon later will blame his lost year of 1974 on fear—fear of getting old, fear of being alone, fear of not having a hit record—and will cite a long succession of people, places, and whiskey bottles. Mostly, he will say, it was waking up and reading about his carrying on in the morning papers.

In July 1974, the immigration appeals board orders Lennon to leave the nation in sixty days or face forcible expulsion. Lennon, dividing his time between New

York and L.A., is not giving up. Jack Anderson reports from Washington that a hundred aliens with worse drug records remain here while the U.S. government hassles John Lennon. If it wasn't manifestly clear before, it seems so now: the Nixon White House has put the screws on Lennon.

Back in New York, Yoko deals with the separation and the bizarre press accounts of John's activities in her own way. "I thought, Oh, poor John," says Yoko. "Part of us was always communicating, though, even during those months . . . we were both sort of exploring, shall we say . . . When he went to L.A., I suggested he go. It was good for both of us to have some space and think about things. To do things independently. We were together twenty-four hours a day for five years."

In January 1975, after a year of boozing with L.A. musicians, hanging out backstage with Elton John, and hearing nothing but bad news on the immigration front, John Lennon returns to New York and Yoko; both of them say there has never really been serious consideration given to a final breakup. As if to cement the resumption of their lives together, they move into the Dakota, an immense co-op on the upper West Side of Manhattan, where celebrities such as Lauren Bacall and Leonard Bernstein find sanctuary. Their relationship seems more solid now than ever. If, as Lennon has said, the separation was like "being kicked out of the nest and being dead," then being back with Yoko is truly being alive again. And in the Dakota, they have found the perfect landmark. Eventually, they will buy up five apartments in the building. "The kind of house I love is a landmark house," explains Yoko. "You know, even if it's falling apart, [there's] something very beautiful about it and . . . we're renovating it, restoring it. I'm cherishing every moment [of living there]." The Lennons will go on to buy numerous other historic houses around the country, mainly on the East Coast. Yoko Ono Lennon says, "We selected the places by just looking at the map and feeling what would be right, there were places I had never been to, but because of numerological considerations [we felt] it would work out well . . ."

In October 1975, after a four-year fight, the U.S. Court of Appeals overturns the deportation order (John Lennon applies for permanent residence status a year later, which he receives without difficulty). Also, in October, Sean Lennon weighs in at 8 pounds 10 ounces. John is actively recording, as he has done throughout the early to mid-1970s, and is still very much a hot press item.

Lennon, who has always feared growing up, says creativity was his means of fighting age—as long as he created music, films, and books, he could block it out. Now, Lennon says he's not so sure. Perhaps, he muses, I've been approaching it from the wrong direction.

The year John Lennon returns to New York and Yoko, ends his battle to live where he wanted to live, fathers his second child, he stops creating, at least in the traditional sense of the word. In 1976 comes the announcement that John Lennon is interested only in being with his family in New York and being a house-husband. To the media, which has thrived on his song and dance for four years, this means he is going underground.

Just how much the lives of John Lennon and Yoko Ono have changed is evident from the decor of their Dakota apartment. One afternoon some carpenters are doing some work in the Lennon living-room walls, which are covered with murals of numerological significance. Yoko instructs the workers to alter a mural of Superman and Superwoman so that the superheroes will wear the faces of John and Yoko, because that is a more positive image for her son. "A piece of me was gone" when Kyoko was taken away, Yoko has said, and John and Yoko aren't going to let it happen again.

In April 1976, *People* magazine has a photo of John Lennon giving the victory sign at the Statue of Liberty. His deportation problems are over and John is no longer a "professional witness" as he awaits his green card. A $42 million libel suit filed against him by contending record labels has likewise been settled in Lennon's favor. His first few weeks as "Frank, Family Man," playing with his infant son, shopping, eating out, and walking through Central Park with Yoko and the baby are giving Lennon a new lease on life. "Life doesn't end," Lennon says, "when you stop subscribing to *Billboard*."

The couple begins to settle into the kind of routine Lennon would have found unimaginable a few years ago. Lennon notes that it took some time to exorcise that part of him that "is performing flea," to give more attention to his "monkish" side. "The fear in the music Business," he will say to *Newsweek,* in an interview in 1980, "is that you don't exist if you're not at Xenon with Andy Warhol . . . it took me a long time to have a live baby [Yoko had several miscarriages through the seventies] and I wanted to give five solid years to Sean. I hadn't seen Julian grow up at all, and now there's a seventeen-year-old on the phone about motorbikes. In other cultures, children don't leave their mother's backs until age two. I think most schools are prisons, a child's thing is wide open and to narrow it down and make him compete in a classroom is a joke. I sent [Sean] to kindergarten and realized I was sending him there to get rid of him. If I don't give him the attention at five, then I'm gonna have to give him double doses in his teenage years."

John and Yoko do everything possible to give Sean a normal life. At three and four years old, he plays with neighborhood youngsters; his father takes him on a Bermuda yacht adventure ("John always had this dream, as an Englishman, about yachting," Yoko says. "He and Sean had a great time"); it is unusual to spot John and Yoko on the street without a stroller or a toddler at their feet.

Sean is a bright youngster, however, and he has questions about his heritage. When the family sits in the car on the way to Tavern on the Green to celebrate Sean's birthday and fans begin kocking on the windows with wild and crazy expressions, Sean inquires why.

Yoko tells him, "Because they love us." That suffices for now.

Meanwhile, Yoko goes off in the morning to do the family business which has spread from a publishing royalty base into real estate, Holstein cattle (an estimated $66 million worth—there is something sacred and mystical in the cow), and dairy farms. John spends a lot of time baking bread, diapering Sean, and discovering who he is. He is aware there is resentment among fans and those in the music business that he has chucked it all for *this*. "I chose not to take the standard options in my business," Lennon tells *Playboy* in 1980, "which are going to Vegas and singing your greatest hits, if you're lucky, or going to hell, which is where Elvis went . . . [You can] become enslaved to the image of what the artist is supposed to do. A lot of artists kill themselves because of it . . . Van Gogh . . . Dylan Thomas."

Lennon and Yoko live a reverse comedy of manners. "To all housewives," Lennon tells *Newsweek*, "I say I now understand what you're screaming about." Lennon's life is built around Sean's meals and bodily functions—Yoko sits in smoky rooms with lawyers and accountants and discusses tax shelters. She arranges a system of personal tithing in which 10 percent of Lennon's annual income goes to charity. During this period, though it is not widely publicized, Lennon and Yoko are active in local charities.

Tens of thousands of New Yorkers have John Lennon stories from the last five years of the seventies. Most of them involve bumping into him getting out of a cab, serving him in a restaurant, or selling him a hat or a coat. (One room at the Dakota residence is said to be hermetically sealed to store Yoko's fur collection.) Though the Lennons are avid shoppers, they are not clotheshorses. On the contrary, they have a distinct garage sale look in public. Their dining preferences tend toward herbs and grains.

The Lennons do a great deal of shopping right on 72d Street. One clothing merchant remembers Lennon walking into his shop trailing a crowd of autograph hounds. "You want me to get rid of them?" he said. "No," shrugged Lennon with a grin. "That's nothing, dear." Lennon seems to enjoy the streets, but not the hassle. "We passed each other one day up on 57th Street," says a fan, "and we looked at each other for an instant. It took me a second to realize who I was seeing and to digest it, by which time Lennon saw what I was thinking and started walking away very fast with his head down. I didn't pursue it, of course."

The Lennons are quiet neighbors and well liked in their building. They do not party, at least not in rock-and-roll circles, and do not attend rock concerts, but regularly attend classical functions around town. Lennon says he is into Muzak, because it adds an environmental element to modern music. "I have no interest in what other [rock] musicians are doing," he says again and again. He also spends some time on the upper East Side, frequenting a bar on 92d Street.

In 1979, after four years of relative mellowness and re-examination of themselves and their relationship, John and Yoko decide to share some of their experiences with the world. Readers of the *New York Times* on May 27 turn to page 20E to find a full-page "Love Letter from John and Yoko to People Who Ask Us What, When And Why." The rambling missive, a hodge-podge of philosophy and kitchen sink surrealism, notes that "if two people like us can do what we are doing with our lives, any miracle is possible!" The letter notes that "the house is getting very comfortable now. Sean is beautiful. The plants are growing, the cats are purring. . . . It's going to be alright! The future of the earth is up to all of us." The letter signs off, "We are all part of the sky, more so than of the ground. Remember, we love you."

To many, it seems like Strawberry Fields, Sgt. Pepper, and Captain Kangaroo revisited.

In the summer of 1980, John and Sean are in Bermuda. The yacht trip is a total success, especially Lennon's heroics during a storm, when he commands the wheel, shouting out sea chanteys "like a crazed Viking." Excited by his seafaring adventures and the first new material he has written in a long time, he calls Yoko in New York and plays her a tape on the phone. She responds by writing her own new material. An album is born.

In September 1980, Lennon is back on the publicity train, and he is better at it than ever, which is saying quite a bit. In the interviews during the last three months of his life, he is all the things he has ever been at any one time: erudite, charming, petty, irrepressible, sweet, gentle, naive, and not embarrassed a whit by any of it. He has dozens of great stories to tell: having to tell Paul McCartney to call before he comes to visit—"I just had a hard day with the baby and I'm worn out": finding out who he was in Hong Kong—"I took time to discover that I was John Lennon before the Beatles"; and much, much more.

John Lennon is once again talking about ART, and people are listening. He talks about walking through the misty mountains of Scotland with an auntie, and smelling the heather. "I thought, Aha, this is the feeling that makes you write or paint." Good, heady stuff.

Only a god, one would think, would embody so many qualities, so many elements from the last two decades. But aside from his singular musical talents, the most arresting quality of John Lennon is his humanness. For it is easy to imagine him cleaning a baby's bottom, cultivating a jar of alfalfa in the kitchen, pushing a stroller down Central Park West, performing the most mundane tasks. Daydreaming constantly. Making love, sometimes hesitantly, sometimes with abandon, like everyone else. As the fan said, the only thing it's impossible to imagine is John Lennon being dead.

4

ALL THE LONELY PEOPLE: THE EARLY YEARS

John Winston Lennon was born on October 9, 1940, in Liverpool, England, to Alfred and Julia Lennon. John had been his grandfather's name, and Winston was tagged on to honor the feisty British prime minister who was busily trying to stave off the doom and destruction of the Second World War. Lennon may have shared combativeness and tenacity with Churchill, but he was none too fond of his middle name: he changed it officially to Ono within days of marrying Yoko.

John's father was a rounder who shipped himself off to sea shortly after John's birth, to reappear many years later when John was a rich and famous Beatle, and to marry a twenty-two-year-old secretary at Apple Records.

John's mother Julia was a dreamy, ethereal woman, unconventional and actively supportive of John's music and nonconformity, but she was unable (or unwilling) to raise a child by herself, and most of John's childhood was spent with Julia's sister Mimi. Though still living in Liverpool, Julia was conspicuous by her absence during much of John's youth. She had just reentered his life, nurturing his talents and taking them seriously, when she was struck and killed by an automobile while crossing the street not far from his home.

In many ways, and on many levels, John never completely recovered from his mother's death. Much of his almost obsessive craving for a secure family life with Yoko, his unshakable resolve to spend his full time with his son Sean, and his private and public habit of referring to the older woman that he married as "Mother" can be traced directly to that July day twenty-six years ago. Having been deserted by both parents, John had finally won one back, only to have her taken away again, this time with a shattering finality that left fissures and ruptures throughout his entire being, havens for the demons that in later life would drive him to both tantrums and transcendence. John had at least one friend who could fully empathize with his loss: James Paul McCartney, currently playing with John in the Quarrymen, a local skiffle band, had lost his own mother two years earlier, an event which was to color his future attitudes almost as much as John's.

Paul's later attempts to surround his relationship with Linda and his children with a seamless aura of idyllic domestic bliss had more in common with John's approach than either of them would be willing to admit. All of this my-family-is-much-more-secure-than-your-family one-upmanship surfaced most clearly during the post-Beatles era. True to form, it was Lennon's songs like "Mother" and "My Mummy's Dead" that pierced the darkened heart of the matter, while McCartney seemed content to warble aural valentines like "My Love" and "Silly Love Songs." "Maybe I'm Amazed" and "Waterfalls" are two revealing exceptions—informal, unstudied works that catch McCartney with his guard down—which revealed a considerably more complicated and sensitive ex-Beatle than the carefree image he usually projects.

By the time of the breakup of the Beatles, both John and Paul were far too self-conscious about convincing each other and the world of their domestic security to reveal the complete range of their feelings about their respective mothers/wives/lovers/children. But if we go back a few years to the Beatles' White Album we find what must be John's most moving tune during his time with the Beatles, the poignant yet ethereal "Julia." "Half of what I say is meaningless/but I say it just to reach you Julia." Like a musical Zen koan, the first lines define and illuminate the inner and outer man. Rarely has an artist so neatly yet comprehensively defined his relationship to himself and the world around him in so few words. "When I cannot sing my heart/I can only speak my mind." And speak he did. Lennon, the brash, boisterous, loud-mouthed, iconoclastic bohemian who railed against an indifferent world, grabbing it by the scruff of the neck and demanding the attention, love, security that he'd been denied as a child. The song's straightforward honesty and vulnerability stand out in vivid contrast to Lennon's usual stridency, humor, and cynicism. The line "Ocean child calls me . . ." is a subtle clue to the true nature of John's feelings, confirming that for him the lines dividing the roles of wife and mother were pretty blurred.

The "ocean child" in question could be the watery, Piscean Julia, but it's also worth nothing that Yoko Ono's name in Japanese means "child of the ocean." Lennon settled any doubts regarding his intentions with "Julia" during his recent *Playboy* interview: "the song ["Julia"] is for her [Julia]—and for Yoko."

Interestingly enough, Paul McCartney's most substantive work with the Beatles dates from approximately the same period and deals with almost exactly the same subject matter. "Lady Madonna" was a tentative probe into a world of true feeling, an emotional reconnaissance—but "Let It Be" and "Hey Jude" were mature masterpieces. "Jude" was written to console Julian, John's son by his first marriage, who was troubled over his somewhat estranged relationship with his father. (One wonders if the profound irony of Paul writing a song to John's son—in effect to John himself —about the feelings of an abandoned child was lost on either of the Beatles. It was a situation they could both certainly feel deeply about.

(Meanwhile Paul had assured the press that it was not the Virgin Mary he was referring to in "Let It Be." As in the case of John's "Julia," McCartney's most moving song was in fact a tribute to his own mother, Mary McCartney.)

Apart from Aunt Mimi, a kind but eminently practical woman who saw little purpose in guitars or writings or drawings, John was raised as a product of the British school system (Quarrybank Grammar School to be exact), which saw even less purpose in guitars, writings, or drawings.

> We put children in boxes. We put old people in boxes. And the rest of us are supposed to be living the good life. But the joke is that children and old people are part of us too. Like I said, [if] you don't give the child attention at five, you're gonna have to give him a double dose at teenage years.
>
> —John Lennon

John needed a double dose and took it out in music, getting attention anyway, anyhow, anytime he could, with a cheap guitar and an expensive attitude:

> I've got a chip on my shoulder
> That's bigger than my feet.
>
> —Lennon/McCartney
> *"I'll Cry Instead"*

It was to be one of a number of crucial threads that would run through Lennon's entire life, helping to mold and shape his music, relationships, and attitudes toward the world at large. Like most things about John Lennon character traits, it had both positive and negative manifestations. Even Lennon's relationship with Allen Klein, the controversial New York lawyer who represented three of the Beatles at the 1970 turn of the decade (and whose stewardship was viewed by many to be either a cause or a symptom of the band's tempestuous breakup), was colored by associations from his childhood. In 1972 Lennon told *Sounds* magazine: "He [Klein] was an orphan, he never had his parents. His mother died when he was a kid and he's as neurotic as me or any other person that's got no parents. He's a capitalist . . . that's his worst sin." Later that year Yoko took much the same stance in an interview with *New Musical Express:* "On personal terms I have nothing against him [Klein]. He's an orphan and I would never discredit him for just that reason."

On June 15, 1955, John's band, the Quarrymen, was playing a church fete at Woolton in Liverpool, a nickel and dime (or shilling and pence) gig that just barely held bands together, paying for beer and bus fare. John's friend Ivan Vaughn showed up with a baby-faced kid, just barely in his teens, who asked to sit in with the band. The newcomer, Paul McCartney, had a good voice and an even better memory (he knew all the words to Eddie Cochran's "Twenty Flight Rock"; Lennon could never remember the words to anything and sang whatever came to mind) and was soon invited to join the band. Three years later, Paul introduced John to George Harrison, who came on as a third guitarist (McCartney was also on guitar), and when Stu Sutcliffe, a childhood friend of John's, won some money in an art contest, he bought a bass and joined the band.

They gigged intermittently around Liverpool as Johnny & the Moondogs, the Nurk Twins, and the Silver Beatles (Beatle being a tip of the hat to Buddy Holly's Crickets—"That'll Be the Day" was the first song Lennon learned to play—although Lennon insisted that a man had appeared to him on a flaming pie and said, "You will be a Beatle with an *a*." All things considered, both versions make sense); and in April 1960, through luck and fate and coincidence, they made the first of four trips to Hamburg, Germany to play a series of dates in dives along the waterfront. The day before leaving, they talked Pete Best into coming along and playing drums with them. (Until then, they'd usually worked without a percussionist, drums being more expensive than guitars—and less transportable—and Liverpool not being the most affluent of cities. "We don't need a drummer," Paul McCartney would tell skeptical club owners. "The rhythm's in the guitars, man!" Those still being the days when Lonnie Donegan and skiffle groups with washboards were popular, many club owners believed him.)

They left Liverpool as provincial journeyman, barely competent but unashamedly enthusiastic, wild with the freedom of a gig in a foreign port, working every night. In Liverpool they were still living with their families; in Hamburg they lived in the back of a movie theater and had no illusions of respectability to maintain. They were encouraged to "make show," to be as rowdy and uncontrollable as possible, onstage as well as off, to get attention by any means possible.

In Hamburg ... we literally worked eight hours a day, it was a full factory day! When we started off we had no audience, so we had to work our asses off to get people in. People would appear at the door of the club while we were onstage, and there'd be nobody at the tables. We used to try to get them in to buy beer. The minute we saw someone we'd kick into "Dancing in the Street" and just rock out, pretending we hadn't seen them. And we'd find we got three of them in, we were like fairground barkers: *see four people —have to get them in!* We eventually sold the club out, which is when we realized it was going to get really big.

—Paul McCartney
Musician: Player & Listener

The constancy of playing night after night after night in front of drunks and rowdies and whores and Hamburg's low-life (and art students) paid off. By the time they returned to Liverpool after their second stay in Hamburg, they were seasoned professionals and, more importantly, they were seasoned rockers. In their absence, the trend in British music had moved away from the raucous, the wild, and the spontaneous, away from Gene Vincent and Little Richard and Carl Perkins, and was now toward the smoother, one-two-three dance-step sound of Cliff Richard, a singer who, in his timidity and mawkishness, made Pat Boone sound positively dangerous. The sailors and the whores and the art students in Hamburg wanted to hear "beat" music, black music, Chuck Berry and Larry Williams and Bo Diddley and Elvis Presley (many of the songs that turned up on Lennon's *Rock 'n' Roll* album were ones he first played in Hamburg), and the Beatles cut their teeth on hard, basic rock and roll, all leather and sweat, far from the pop pablum of the BBC.

In Liverpool, they began a series of day and night engagements at the Cavern Club, "a cellar full of noise" that became for the Beatles and the whole Mersey scene what New York's CBGB would later become for the New Wave crowd.

> I wouldn't know because I wasn't in the audience at the Cavern, I was onstage, but visually it looked the same. The only passing thought I had about it was that instead of having Brian Epstein come and say, "Stop spitting and chewing and cursing the audience," that now, twenty-five years later, that was the act.
>
> —John Lennon
> *Newsweek*

Along with the constant gigs at the Cavern, Lennon (who had always written and drawn his own comic books when he was growing up) began writing for the local Liverpool music tabloid *Merseybeat,* contributing odd stories, columns (as "The Beatcomber"), and bizarre classified ads.

Meanwhile, in the Whitechapel district of Liverpool, a young record store owner named Brian Epstein began receiving inquiries about a record called "My Bonnie," by the Beatles, Epstein's pride and joy was a device he had installed in his store whereby little strings dangled from empty record jackets when albums needed to be reordered, and he prided himself on his knowledge of records and his ability to fill any order, however small. He started making inquiries, and found that the record had never been released in the U.K. It had been recorded in Hamburg the previous spring with the Beatles backing singer Tony Sheridan and released in Germany on Polydor. The single was a rock reworking of the old chestnut "My Bonnie Lies Over the Ocean," part of the inane trend of arranging tired standards as "beat" songs that Carl Perkins began with a rock-and-roll version of "Annie Laurie."

Epstein learned that they were a local group and began haunting the Cavern, turning up at more and more performances until he made up his mind to manage them. The prospect of being a manager, of some sort of creative involvement, delighted him; a failed actor, he had retreated into his family's furniture business, had expanded the business to include records, and had eventually opened up his own (very successful) record store. Business was prospering, but he was easily bored, and he had been channeling all his creative energies into writing columns for local music magazines, devising his own Top Ten charts for the walls of his store, and dangling small bits of string from empty record jackets. If nothing else, the Beatles would be a change.

He immediately insisted they clean up their image, discarding the leather jackets and jeans for tailored suits (collarless), shortening their sets to what he considered their best numbers, and eliminating some of their more yobish tendencies, like munching sandwiches on stage and shouting and conversing with members of the audience between songs. Epstein was determined to fashion the Beatles into a commercially viable entity, yet he was always sensitive to their needs and their feelings. John's relationship with Brian was characteristically ambivalent: John was the oldest, the most outrageous, and the one most inclined to cause trouble, to bridle at Brian's suggestions, to disagree out of sheer whim and perversity. In Hamburg, John had amused himself by insulting the patrons of the clubs they played in calling them all Nazis, and on at least one occasion appearing with a toilet seat hung round his neck.

A diplomat by nature, Paul had always relied on his charm to get through difficulties; he allied himself with Epstein in his bid to sanitize and commercialize their music and image.

John became increasingly resentful of what he felt was their conspiracy to sell out in order to make it big. The money was rolling in, but their music, according to Lennon, was dying. At the same time, Lennon realized that he needed Epstein's help in containing his more irresponsible tendencies.

"... Paul and Epstein did have to cover up a lot for me. I'm not putting Paul down, and I'm not putting Brian down. They did a good job in containing my personality from causing too much trouble."

—John Lennon

Epstein's overhaul of the Beatles quickly paid off in more bookings in larger and more prestigious halls, and after a number of auditions and false starts and rejections, he landed them a contract with E.M.I. George Martin, who had signed them to the label, was reasonably impressed with the Beatles, though groups were not in fashion (there was almost always a lead singer, a "personality" with a faceless backing group), but was more impressed with the quiet and reserved style of their manager, a change from the West End loudmouths he usually had to deal with.

At this point, Pete Best had been unceremoniously dumped as their drummer and been replaced by Ringo, and Stu Sutcliffe had left the band to stay and live in Hamburg, leaving bass chores to McCartney. "Love Me Do," their first single, was a moderate hit, but

"Please Please Me," released in January '63, quickly hit number one on the British charts.

There was this incredible excitement. So we knew something we were doing must have been right. By the time we started playing tours it really didn't surprise us anymore—though we were still thrilled by it all. When we were on the Chris Montez tour he was on the top of the bill; halfway through they switched it and put us on top. It was embarrassing as hell for him, I mean what could we say to him, Sorry, Chris? He took it well and stuff, but we expected it by then. Everywhere we'd gone it seemed to work. The British papers were saying, "What's left to do? You've conquered everything. And we'd say *AMERICA!!*

—Paul McCartney
Musician: Player & Listener

No British pop group had ever made it big in the States. Frank Ifield had had a hit with "I Remember You," as had Lonnie Donegan with his novelty record "Does Your Chewing Gum Lose Its Flavor on the Bedpost Overnight?" but that was about it. Even Cliff Richard, Britain's favorite son, had failed miserably when he tried to crack the American music scene. It all went the other way. America had Ray Charles, James Brown, the Ronettes and the Crystals and Dion and Del Shannon. What did they need with English musicians?

Epstein's first reception in the States was chilly, but quiet perseverence (and the fact that Ed Sullivan had seen evidence of Beatlemania, riots at airports and all, on a recent trip to London) garnered them top billing on the Sullivan show.

On February 9, 1964, John, Paul, George and Ringo made their American television debut, opening with "All My Loving," "Till There Was You," and "She Loves You," returning to encore with "I Saw Her

Standing There" and "I Want to Hold Your Hand."

And everything exploded. That night in living rooms all over America, a generation discovered its birthright. It was an awakening and a liberation on a massive scale, almost impossible to explain to those not touched by it.

I personally think that in America there was a standard way of doing things. The only freaky people were the Hollywood writers, jazz musicians and pop stars—but even they were tied to a framework. Meanwhile, we had cooked up this whole new British thing; we had a long time to work it all out and make our mistakes in Hamburg with almost no one watching. We were very different, having taken all these American influences and stewed them up in British way . . . we'd distilled our stuff down to an essence, so we weren't just coming on as any old band—we had our own totally new identities. The thing we did —which I always think new groups should take as a bit of advice—was that we were cheeky enough to say that we wouldn't go to the States without a number one record there . . . there was a lot of careful thought behind it.

—Paul McCartney
Musician: Player & Listener

The music itself was an amalgam of styles, with bits borrowed and reprocessed from Chuck Berry, Little Richard, the Everly Brothers, Smokey & the Miracles, and even show tunes. But it was more than a collection of American rhythm-and-blues styles thrown together. The Beatles had absorbed and synthesized their influences, and at the heart of their music was a compositional originality and sophistication all their own.

When we started the Beatles, John and I sat down and wrote about fifty songs, out of which "Love Me Do," I think, is the only one that got published. Those songs weren't very good because we were trying to find the next beat—*the next new sound*. The minute we stopped trying to FIND that new beat, the newspapers started saying it was US; and we'd found we'd discovered the new sound without even trying.

—Paul McCartney
Musician: Player & Listener

Even the eminently respectable and conservative *Times* of London (which felt compelled to warn readers that three of the four Beatles played guitars that were electronically amplified and plucked in a rather unusual manner) rhapsodized about the "pandiatonic clusters" and "Aeolian cadences" in their songs, terms that Lennon and McCartney, who had had no formal musical training, found amusing if somewhat incomprehensible.

Perhaps the most remarkable aspect of what came to be called Beatlemania was that it blossomed from a rumor to a full-fledged cultural phenomenon in little more than one month. One moment no one had heard of them, the next they were everywhere, with songs of theirs competing with other songs of theirs on the charts ("I Want to Hold Your Hand," and "She Loves You," and "Love Me Do," and "Please Please Me," and "Do You Want to Know a Secret?" battled each other on the radio that February in 1964), photo spreads in *Life* magazine, endless (eminently quotable) press conferences, more spots on the Ed Sullivan show, concerts at Carnegie Hall, and, through it all, the inane Beatle jokes and Beatle wigs. If their music—and their manager—got them to America, it turned out to be the jokes and the Beatle wigs which made them a household word. And the jokes were soon forgotten.

That spring, in the midst of the frenzy, they started work on their first film, *A Hard Day's Night,* shot on location in Liverpool. Lennon was incensed by what he felt was the clever but pointless banter of the script, and fought for a more realistic presentation. Screenwriter Alun Owen had picked out certain mannerisms and character traits for each member that (Lennon felt) made caricatures of the individual Beatles, though his early portraits stuck with them: John the witty rebel, Paul the charmer, Ringo cute and bungling, and George eager and somewhat airy. Their reactions to the film showed that, whatever his shortcomings, Owen hadn't strayed too far from the mark: Paul good-naturedly accepted it as another job, John complained, George was vague, and Ringo smiled.

The film was a smash, with the Beatles constantly compared with the Marx brothers (and a brilliant acting career predicted for Ringo). Orchestral versions of Beatles songs (mostly pointless) began appearing, and no less than Aaron Copland and Leonard Bernstein were touting Lennon and McCartney as brilliant and original composers. The boom continued: More singles ("I Feel Fine," "Eight Days a Week," "Ticket to Ride"), more tours, another movie (*Help!*), and a growing sense that time and frenzy and money were never going to stop. But on a deeper level the Beatles, especially John, were about to enter a period of questioning and reassessment. As John Lennon would admit years later, the song "Help" was more than a catchy movie tune. It was a genuine cry from the heart.

5

STRAWBERRY FIELDS

The music business today is a multibillion-dollar industry and recording performers are often considered artists with a capital *A*. But that wasn't true in the mid-sixties. George Martin, for example, was a staff producer for E.M.I., working straight salary, with no percentages of profit on the albums sold. He received less money for producing *Help!, Rubber Soul,* and *Revolver* combined than a good session guitarist would now make on one album project.

If a current artist releases two albums and two or three singles a year, she is considered extraordinarily prolific; one album a year for someone considered an Artist is normal, and two years between records is not unusual. But in the mid-sixties, no one worried about "Art." They worried about turning out product: you didn't wait two years, you waited two weeks (there was still a sense then that the boom might subside, that within the month or the year twist or calypso or cha-cha records might be back in fashion).

Between July 1965 and August 1966, the Beatles released six singles in the U.S.:

"Help"/"I'm Down"
"Yesterday"/"Act Naturally"
"We Can Work It Out"/"Day Tripper"
"Nowhere Man"/"What Goes On"

"Paperback Writer"/"Rain"
"Yellow Submarine"/"Eleanor Rigby"

four albums:

>   *Help*
>   *Rubber Soul*
>   *"Yesterday" . . . and Today*
>   *Revolver*

and one film:

>   *Help!*

They also toured Britain, Germany, Japan, the Philippines, and America and performed on a number of TV shows.

This body of work, considering that it includes much of the best work they ever produced, is staggering. No wonder Lennon couldn't remember which album was recorded first, *Revolver* or *Rubber Soul;* time was completely telescoped.

>   I have a very good memory, but I say two months, it means six months, you know? Because I've never lived on a real schedule.
>
>   —John Lennon

Rubber Soul was the first album on which the Beatles existed and took full control, both in the studio (where they began to actively collaborate with George Martin) and in the songs (it was the first album on which they'd written all the material). The sound and feel was very influenced by the Byrds (accoustic and twelve-string guitars abounded) and Bob Dylan, particularly Lennon's "Norwegian Wood," the story of an extramarital affair.

Lennon was also beginning to write first-person music, songs that related directly to him (not his idea of what a pop song should be or was supposed to be), and "In My Life" and "Girl" were very new kinds of songs for him.

We were just getting better, technically, and musically, that's all. Finally we took over the studio. In the early days, we had to take what we were given, we didn't know how you can get more bass. We were learning the technique on *Rubber Soul*. We were more precise about making the album, that's all, and we took over the cover and everything.

—John Lennon

There was a backlash against the Beatles in the summer of 1966. John's remark about the Beatles being more popular than Jesus had angered a lot of people who never bothered to see its context, "Paperback Writer" hadn't been as popular as the preceding single, and, basically, they'd been on top too long and a lot of people were waiting for them to fall on their faces.

So the revolver in the title of their new album was supposedly aimed at all their detractors and critics. But not music critics—pop music was still not written about seriously as anything other than teen fodder, though that would all change. At about the same time *Revolver* was released, Richard Goldstein began writing "Pop Eye," a thoughtful column in New York's *Village Voice*, and Paul Williams had just begun publishing *Crawdaddy*, the first rock magazine.

Just to show you how wrong one can be: I was in Germany on tour just before *Revolver* came out. I started listening to the album, and I got really down because I thought the whole thing was out of tune. Everyone had to reassure me that it was okay.

—Paul McCartney
Musician: Player and Listener

If *Rubber Soul* had made the Beatles respectable, serious, and talented musicians, *Revolver* totally blew the lid off. They were growing faster than anyone's ears could keep up with. They'd experimented with sound before (the feedback introduction to "I Feel Fine," the backward section of "Rain," the sitar on "Norwegian Wood") but never so daringly, and never in such a way that the idea, the experiment, and the song merged into one.

Language and song is to me, apart from being pure vibrations, just like trying to describe a dream. And because we don't have telepathy or whatever it is, we try and describe the dream to each other, to verify to each other what we know, what we believe is inside each other. But no matter how you say it, it's never how you want to say it. Because the words are irrelevant.

Why do I have to explain what sound is? I mean we all sit by the sea and listen to it. But do we say, "This sea is good because it's reminiscent of childhood experience when we were at the seaside" or "It's like your mother's water" or anything like that? People just lie in fields and listen to birds and nobody says a thing.

—John Lennon

The presumption behind "Tomorrow Never Knows," with the birds and the backward tapes and loops (Lennon had originally wanted to use monks chanting as the backing, but it proved impractical), coupled with lyrics taken from *The Tibetan Book of the Dead,* was terrifying.

> Turn off your mind,
> Relax, and float downstream
> It is not dying
> It is not dying.

"Tomorrow Never Knows"
—Lennon/McCartney

The sound was dense, the lyrics almost impenetrable, but the import was undeniable, and when it came on the radio it sounded like nothing else in the world. Dylan's *Blonde on Blonde* was released the same summer, about the same time, and it felt like he and the Beatles, particularly Lennon, were having long conversations over the airwaves in some preternatural haze of Zen and methedrine, trading secrets and dark glasses.

> Lay down all thoughts,
> Surrender to the void
> It is shining
> It is shining.
>
> —Lennon/McCartney
> "Tomorrow Never Knows"

The Beatles were embraced wildly by the art crowd, the avant-garde, and the intellectuals, though there was always a small sense of confusion, or conflict: what was this man who was singing about the oversoul doing jumping up and down on stages around the world singing "Twist and Shout"?

The touring did stop, but it was for different reasons. The Beatles were learning to take an active interest in recording, trying out different sounds, different instruments, speeding up and slowing down voices and creating total aural environments, and none of this could be duplicated onstage. They had no control onstage, could barely hear each other, and the audience was some screaming intangible force, seemingly miles away, a sea of arms waving madly. But records were a different story.

I like records. I really do. With all the performers I ever saw, from Little Richard to Jerry Lee [Lewis], I was always slightly disappointed. I preferred the record. Because they never sounded exactly like the record. You know I like "Whole Lotta Shaking," the take that he did in 1956, on the record. I'm not interested in the variation on a theme. When Gene Vincent did "Be Bop a Lula" in Hamburg, he didn't do it the same. It was *not*

"Be Bop a Lula." It was a thrill to meet Gene Vincent and see Gene Vincent, but it was not "Be Bop a Lula." I'm a record fan.

—John Lennon

There were a lot of reasons for them to stop touring, but despite the adulation and overintellectualization of the avant-garde, they had no conflicts reconciling the new and expanding music they were playing with rock and roll.

There is nothing conceptually better than rock and roll. No group, Beatles, Dylan, or Stones, have ever improved on "Whole Lotta Shaking" for my money. Or maybe I'm like our parents: that's my period and I dig it, and I'll never leave it.

—John Lennon

They'd been riding a whirlwind since 1963, and as wonderful and dizzying as the ride was, it was no longer necessary. The constant succession of hotels and airports and automatic frenzy had become numbing, and the music played onstage had become as automatic as the hysteria, craftsmanship pure and simple, nothing more, nothing less.

Somewhere around then they must have realized two things: that they were very rich men, and would remain rich for life; and that they were artists and in control of their own work, with no one to answer to.

If there is such a thing as a genius, I am one, and if there isn't, I don't care. I didn't become something when the Beatles made it or when you heard about me. I've been like this all me life.

—John Lennon
Rolling Stone, No 75
© 1970 Straight Arrow Publishers

That fall of 1966, with his new freedom, Lennon went off to Spain to act in *How I Won The War*. The fact that it was an antiwar film and that Richard Lester, who had directed *A Hard Day's Night* and *Help!*, was in charge had drawn him to the project, but it was a mediocre film and Lennon felt he was being used as little more than an extra. But while there, on the beach at Almeria, he wrote "Strawberry Fields Forever," a strange and brilliant rendition that combined the best features of "Tomorrow Never Knows" and "She Said She Said" pushed to even further extremes.

Strawberry Fields was a house in Liverpool near where he'd grown up after moving from Penny Lane (the address on the other side of the single) and moving in with his aunt. Lennon went to garden parties there when he was a boy, and the song is thick with a strange sense of misplaced childhood, like a fairy tale that's about to turn on itself. Like those of Lewis Carroll and Edward Lear and E. T. A. Hoffman, Lennon's childhood evocations are gentle but never sweet, and almost always filled with a very real sense of danger and the perverse.

To fit the lopsided, conversational mood of the piece, George Martin invented an entirely new language in the studio. The song pulsed, cascaded into whirlygigs and steam organs, and moved into free time, with voices that seemed to burrow up and under each other. If it wasn't their most experimental production ("I Am the Walrus" probably was), it was the most spontaneous and the most exuberant.

The sense of production Martin invented with "Strawberry Fields Forever" served them well in the months ahead when they began recording *Sgt. Pepper's Lonely Hearts Club Band* and tried to make a record that sounded like what LSD felt like. But before *Sgt. Pepper*, and before "Strawberry Fields" was released, Lennon had met and fallen in love with Yoko Ono. And everything changed.

I'd been told about this "event"—this avant-garde artist coming from America. I was looking

around the gallery and I saw this ladder and
climbed up and got a look in this spyglass on the
top of the ladder—you feel like a fool—and it
just said, YES. Now, at the time, all the avant-
garde was smash the piano with a hammer and
break the sculpture and anti-, anti-, anti-, anti-,
anti-. It was all boring, negative crap, you know.
And just that YES made me stay in a gallery full
of apples and nails.

There was a sign that said HAMMER A NAIL
IN, so I said, "Can I hammer a nail in?" But
Yoko said no, because the show wasn't opening
until the next day. But the owner came up and
whispered to her, "Let him hammer a nail in.
You know, he's a millionaire. He might buy it."
And so there was this little conference, and finally
she said, "OK, you can hammer a nail in for five
shillings." So smartass says, "Well, I'll give you
an imaginary five shillings and hammer an imaginary nail in." And that's when we really met.
That's when we locked eyes, and she got it, and I
got it, and, as they say in all the interviews we do,
the rest is history.

—John Lennon
© 1980 *Playboy*

The only thing worse than a genius is a genius in
love. John Lennon fell madly in love with Yoko Ono,
and he brought all of the genius and talent of his songs
and his pictures and his writing and his heart to that
love.

We met, we had to decide what our common
goal was. We had one thing in common—we were
in love. But love is just a gift, and it doesn't
answer everything and it's like a precious plant
that you have to nurture and look after and all
that.

—John Lennon
© 1971 Straight Arrow Publishers

If Lennon had been looking for new sides of himself when he went to Spain to act in "How I Won the War" or in the new, more experimental songs he was trying, if he was at all dissatisfied with the pop music world and the routine he had fallen into with the Beatles and was looking for some new source of inspiration, he found all of this in Yoko.

It wasn't that she inspired the songs. She inspired *me.*

—John Lennon
© 1980 *Playboy*

Even for a public personality, it was the most public of romances, though it was approached with such a fanatical romantic innocence that it couldn't help but be touching. Here was this loud-mouthed lunatic millionaire pop star, a member of the most successful rock group in the world, acting like a fool . . . and enjoying the fact that he was acting like a fool.

It was genuinely touching; but not everyone was touched. Yoko was oriental, seven years older than John, and an artist in her own right, a woman—not a girl—with her own life. Any one of those factors may have been strange and threatening to a public that feels that it owns its heroes. The combination of all of them was devastating. As Charles Alverson wrote several years later in *Rolling Stone:*

Yoko is all passion and unguarded innocence, but she acts as a magnet for whatever scorn and hatred the [public] might like to heap on John if they didn't love him.

The Beatles were no more enthralled with Yoko than the public was, though initially they were probably just confused and uninterested. The Beatles were the Beatles and their girlfriends and their wives were their girlfriends and their wives. It all seemed clear (well, maybe not VERY clear—these were, after all, the early days of acid and things were cosmic and psychadelic and magical, but not necessarily clear). John was bringing Yoko around to the studio and acting as if she were his partner, his collaborator. As if she were— God forbid—a Beatle.

> I would have expanded the Beatles and broken them and gotten their pants off and stopped them being God, but it didn't work.
>
> —John Lennon

Lennon retreated into a life with Yoko, using his talents to make highly conceptual films with her, beginning a collaboration on the recording of experimental, private tapes, more artifacts than records, which were ultimately released as *Unfinished Music No. 1.— Two Virgins*.

That winter, though, the Beatles began work on *Sgt. Pepper's Lonely Hearts Club Band*.

> People just have this dream about *Sgt. Pepper*. It was good for then, but it wasn't that spectacular when you look back on it. I prefer some of the tracks off the double album and some of the tracks off *Abbey Road*. When you think back on *Pepper*, what do you remember? Just "A Day in the Life." You know, I go for individual songs, not for whole albums.
>
> —John Lennon

It's hard to see the album through Lennon's eyes, from the inside. From the outside, it's impossible to tell whether the age created the Beatles or the Beatles created the age, but *Sgt. Pepper* was perfectly in synch with the mood of the summer of 1967, and defined it if not created it.

It's just the beginning. There is no end.

—Paul McCartney
Hit Parader Magazine

We're the Beatles, and it's a little scene we're playing and we're pretending to be Beatles like Harold Wilson is pretending to be prime minister.

—George Harrison, 1967
Hit Parader Magazine

I had this idea that it was going to be an album of another band that wasn't us—we'd just imagine all the time that it wasn't us playing. It was just a nice little device to give us some distance on the album.

—Paul McCartney
Musician: Player and Listener

It was a time of masks and doors behind doors, nothing was quite what it seemed (and then again, maybe it was). The pretty nurse from Penny Lane acts as if she's in a play, but she actually *is* in a play. Life goes on within you and without you (not just outside yourself, but *without* you, when you're not around, life's still going on, Jack.) The record honeycombed the summer with a cosmic sunniness, with the sense that you could follow your psyche to the end of the rainbow, and when you got there all your friends would be there waiting for you, all your friends and most especially your old friends the Beatles.

Rumors spread that there actually *was* a Pepperland, an emerald city of rock and roll and Owsley, and that if you added up all the numbers mentioned in *Sgt. Pepper* (the twenty years since the good sergeant had taught the band to play, the ten thousand holes in Blackburn Lancashire, the five o'clocks and nine o'clocks of "She's Leaving Home") and added these to the combined ages of the Beatles, the number of people on the front cover, and the serial number of the record itself, you would have a seven-digit number—a telephone number! And if you dialed this number, someone would come and spirit you off to Pepperland. People who told the story most convincingly always mentioned some close friend of theirs who had dialed the number and never-been-seen-again.

Lennon, as usual, cut through the optimism and cheerfulness with his own fears and confessions.

> I used to be cruel to my woman
> I beat her and kept her apart from the things
> that she loved.
>
> —Lennon/McCartney
> "Getting Better," 1967

> I used to be cruel to my woman. I couldn't express myself and I hit. I fought men and I hit women. That is why I am always on about peace, you see. It is the most violent people who got for love and peace. I am a violent man who has learned not to be violent and regrets his violence. I will have to be a lot older before I can face in public how I treated women as a youngster.
>
> —John Lennon
> © 1980 *Playboy*

And "A Day in the Life," otherworldly and still chilling, with the sense of a symphony gone mad, and the enormous final chord, aching into what seemed like eternity.

Aside from a qualified pan in the *New York Times* (which still called "A Day in the Life" a masterpiece), the album was praised to the skies, the Beatles appeared on the cover of *Time,* and the music was unavoidable; it filled the air like a national anthem.

> I think we're getting influenced by ourselves.
>
> —Paul McCartney
> *Hit Parader*

Sgt. Pepper was quickly followed by "All You Need Is Love," one of Lennon's best utopian fantasies. Despite the elaborate production (and the inclusion of motifs from old Beatles songs, "Greensleeves," and anything else available), the cockeyed brass section and the hesitant lead guitar (with its faint stutter) seemed spontaneous and overwhelmingly charming after the planned perfection of *Sgt. Pepper,* and the song was everywhere. If not an anthem, it was, at least, a national mantra.

> All you need is love
> All you need is love
> All you need is love, love,
> Love is all you need.
>
> —Lennon/McCartney
> "All You Need Is Love," 1967

The Beatles had other mantras on their minds, though. George's fascination with Indian music had led to an interest in Indian religion, and his then wife, Patti, had become a member of the Spiritual Regeneration Movement and learned about transcendental meditation and about Maharishi Mahesh Yogi, an Indian guru. (In India, as Lennon has since pointed out, they don't have pop stars, they have gurus. And the Maharishi was a very big pop star.)

George talked the others into going to a lecture that the Maharishi was giving, and they were impressed enough to want to go on a weekend retreat with the Maharishi in Wales (although a retreat that included Mick Jagger, Marianne Faithfull, hordes of fans, cameramen, reporters, and newsmen. was probably more of a circus than a time of spiritual regeneration).

In any event, the retreat was shortened. On Sunday, August 27, 1967, word arrived that their manager, Brian Epstein, had been found dead in his London apartment.

Newsclips from that time show Lennon in a state of shock, looking, with his glasses and his long hair and his sideburns, like a haunted sheep.

"What are you going to do now?" a reporter asks him.

"I don't know," he says. "I don't know."

After Brian died, we collapsed. Paul took over and supposedly led us. But what is leading us when we went round in circles? We broke up then. That was the disintegration.

—John Lennon

Lennon was always considered the Beatles' leader—the most daring as well as the most actively articulate—but even before Epstein's death, John had begun to lose interest in the day-to-day workings of the group, spending most of his time with Yoko, and Paul had begun to take over the leadership. The concept of *Sgt. Pepper* was Paul's, and so was the idea of the TV film that became *Magical Mystery Tour*. It was to be a Christmas present to their fans (it was shown on the BBC on December 26), but most of all it was to show that the Beatles were still the Beatles, with or without Brian Epstein.

It didn't work.

We goofed really.

—Paul McCartney
Musician: Player and Listener

Meant as an impressionist collage that would be a film's equivalent of *Sgt. Pepper* (something of a cross between the projected Stones' Rock 'n' Roll Circus and the dream life of Walter Mitty), it wound up a psychedelic hodge-podge of posturing and self-indulgence. It's never been shown in the States—outside of college campuses and occasional Beatles festivals—and is generally acknowledged to be a failure.

Lennon's only real contribution to the film was "I Am the Walrus," the only really first-rate song to come out of the movie. Using an extension of the recording techniques that he and George Martin had perfected on "Strawberry Fields Forever" and also used on "Being for the Benefit of Mr. Kite," they created a strange and lumbering song, part nightmare, part incantation, part naughty children's song.

Whenever the nightmare gets too abstract, too far afield, it returns to the real nightmare, the one real fact at the center of the song: "I'm crying."

In early 1968, shortly after *Magical Mystery Tour* was aired (and panned), the Beatles announced the formation of Apple Corp., a utopian company that would produce records and films, patent magic inventions (an inventor named Magic Alex was hired and magically disappeared), sell hippie clothing, and make people's dreams come true. On February 24, Paul McCartney told the *Evening Standard:* "Instead of trying to amass money for the sake of it, we're setting up a business concern at Apple—rather like a Western Communism . . . we've got all the money we need. I've got the house and the cars and all the things money can buy."

John added: "The aim of the company isn't a stack of gold teeth in the bank. We've done that bit. It's more of a trick to see if we can get artistic freedom within a business structure; to see if we can create things and sell them without charging three times our cost."

In the midst of setting up Apple, the Beatles left for a short stay in India, studying with the Maharishi, and also released a new single, "Lady Madonna." Having taken elaborate productions as far as they could logically (and illogically) go, it was a return to very basic rock and roll (a sound which could be reproduced live—which got people wondering and hoping), and a taste of the less refined, more direct sound they would go for on the White Album. "Lady Madonna" was, by the way, the last Beatles record released on Capitol . . . all later records came out on Apple.

The trip to India was not as long or as rewarding as they'd hoped. Ringo returned after ten days (he was homesick, even though he'd brought his wife and a number of cans of baked beans with him to India),

Paul after a month, and after two months Lennon convinced George Harrison that the Maharishi was a sham, and they returned to London. "Sexy Sadie," who "made a fool of everyone," was Lennon's description of the Maharishi.

> We gave her everything we owned just to sit at her table.

> —Lennon/McCartney
> "Sexy Sadie," 1968

That spring, amid more activity setting up Apple, Lennon made a trip to New York and, on a televised interview, called the Vietnam War "a piece of insanity." More and more involved in the peace movement, Lennon was convinced that peace could be hustled and sold the same way records were, and he determined to use his name and his celebrity to spread a gospel of goodwill, peace, and optimism.

> What we've got to do is keep hope alive. Because without it we'll sink.

> —John Lennon

> The whole future of the earth seems to me to depend on the awakening of our faith in the future.

> —Pierre Teilhard de Chardin

On June 15, 1968, with great ceremony, John and Yoko planted two acorns at Coventry Cathedral. They later sent acorns to all the world leaders as a symbol of (the possibility, at least, of) hope and peace.

A month later, the cartoon feature *Yellow Submarine* premiered, a harmless piece of fluff that had next to nothing to do with the Beatles. Of the four new (contractually obligatory) songs, only Lennon's "Hey Bulldog" had any substance or bite.

> Some kind of innocence
> is measured out in years.
>
> —Lennon/McCartney
> "Hey Bulldog," 1968

But none of this mattered once the new single was released.

I happened to be driving out to see Cynthia Lennon, I think it was just after she and John had broken up, and I was quite matey with Julian [their son]. And I was going out in me car just vaguely singing this song, and it was like, "Hey, Jules, don't make it bad/take a sad song..." And then I thought a better name was Jude. A bit more country and western for me.

—Paul McCartney

The flip side, "Revolution," was even more remarkable and, at the same time, very controversial.

I wanted to put out what I felt about revolution: I had been thinking about it up in the hills in India. I still had this "God will save us" feeling about it, it's going to be all right, but that's why I did it, I wanted to talk, I wanted to say my piece about revolutions. I wanted to tell you, or whoever listens, to communicate, to say, "What do you say? This is what I say." On one version I said, "Count me in" about violence, in or out, because I wasn't sure. But the version we put out said, "Count me out," because I don't fancy a violent revolution happening all over. I don't want to die; but I began to think about what else can happen, you know; it seems inevitable.

—John Lennon

Lennon was in the news constantly during the fall of 1968. Cynthia Lennon filed for divorce and won custody of their son Julian. The album he and Yoko had put together, *Unfinished Music No. 1—Two Virgins,* featuring a nude picture of themselves on the cover, was released and immediately held up to scorn and ridicule. (30,000 copies of it were later seized in New Jersey as pornographic material.)

Lennon was too smart not to have anticipated this sort of a reaction, but he had left himself vulnerable nevertheless and felt hurt if not betrayed by the outrage and the insults, especially as they were mostly aimed at Yoko. People still did not accept them as a couple, and Yoko was "a magnet for whatever scorn or hatred the [public] might like to heap on John if they didn't love him." (Charles Alverson, reprise.)

And injury was added to insult. On October 18, 1968, police raided the flat in Montagu Square, Marylebone, where John and Yoko were living and charged them with possession of cannabis. John claimed sole responsibility, and they were released on bail; John later pleaded guilty and paid a fine of 150 pounds (about $400), but there were other damages. Yoko had been pregnant at the time of the raid and, in all the stress and confusion, she lost the child. And the drug charge, slight as it was, became the focus of Lennon's protracted battle with the U.S. immigration authorities when, in the early Seventies, they tried to deport him as an undesirable alien.

> You know I'd give you everything I've got
>   for a litttle peace of mind.
> You know I'd give you everything I've got
>   for a litttle peace of mind.
>
> —Lennon/McCartney
> "I'm So Tired," 1968

If the White Album (released on two LPs as *The Beatles*) was a return to simplicity, to very clear and undistorted production, it was also a removal of the masks everyone had tried on around the time of *Sgt. Pepper*. The songs weren't the only things left naked.

Lennon, always the most unguarded, had written most of his songs while in India, learning to meditate.

But instead of tranquil, pastoral songs of inner light and peace, they were clear, direct screams of pain and frustration.

It ["I'm So Tired"] reminds me of how many changes John has gone through since he was the plump, cheeky leader of the Fab Four. Jesus Christ, *Sgt. Pepper* leading the children's crusade through Disneyland; a voyage to India as victims of their own propaganda; Apple, a citadel of Mammon . . . even two years ago, the image of Lennon as a martyr would have seemed ludicrous, but as his trial (the aforementioned trial for possession of cannabis resin) approaches, a gaunt, spiritual John hardly recognizable as his former self emerges. This metamorphosis has taken place only at the cost of an incredible amount of energy, and the weariness of this song seems to fall like the weight of gravity.

—David Dalton, 1968

"Julia was a love song to his dead mother (and to Yoko) that seems a small, pleasant ballad until the hurt and despair comes pouring through:

When I cannot sing my heart
I can only speak my mind
Julia.

—Lennon/McCartney
"Julia," 1968

And as much as "Yer Blues" is a parody of the self-indulgent, electric blues that had become so fashionable in the late sixties, the hurt is still obvious. And though she gives as if she's in a play, she is anyway. A parody of pain can still contain pain.

My mother was of the sky,
My father was of the earth.

But I am of the universe
And you know what it's worth.

—Lennon/McCartney
"Yer Blues," 1968

(As late as 1980, Lennon still thought of himself as
of the universe, or at least beyond state and border.
When preparing for the January 1980 *Playboy* interview, Yoko Ono mentioned a number of conditions
and rules that had to be adhered to. The interviewer
tried to remind her that he was experienced and had
interviewed any number of famous people, among
them President Carter. "People like Jimmy Carter represent only their country," she replied. "John and I
represent the world.")

Yes I'm lonely, wanna die
If I ain't dead already.

—Lennon/McCartney
"Yer Blues"

The starkness was sometimes unbearable. With the
masks down, the Beatles no longer recognized one
another's faces (much less their own, sometimes), and
for the first time they no longer seemed to be a group,
a whole much greater than the sum of its parts, but
four very separate individuals.

The White Album. That was the tension album. We were all in the midst of the psychedelic
thing, or just coming out of it. In any case, it was
weird. Never before had we recorded with beds in
the studio and people writing for hours on end;
business meetings and all that. There was a lot of
friction during that album . . . we were about to
break up. And that was just tense in itself.

—Paul McCartney
Musician: Player and Listener

Part of that tension was financial. Apple was losing money hand over first. The Apple boutique had already closed, with close to $50,000 worth of stock having been given away, and at Apple's main offices, both Paul and John had taken turns coming in on a daily basis and overseeing the place. But neither one of them had the skill or the temperament of a businessman, and the money was simply floating away.

It could never make sense to me to have money and yet think the way I thought. I had to give it away or lose it. I gave a lot of money away, which is, you know, one way of losing it; and the other way is disregarding it and not paying attention to it, not taking responsibility for what I really was, which is a guy with a lot of money, you know.

—John Lennon

It became apparent to all of them that whatever guilt was being assuaged by their losses at Apple, they could no longer be taken for a collective ride. Their coffers were not as bottomless as they had hoped. In early 1969, Lennon told *Disc and Music Echo*: "Apple is losing money. If it carries on like this, we'll be broke in six months."

Enter Allen Klein. Business manager for the Rolling Stones and reportedly one sharp (and not necessarily honest) son of a bitch, he offered to put their financial fracas back in order and begin making some money for them. McCartney didn't like him or trust him, and tried to bring in John Eastman (his soon-to-be father-in-law), an aristocratic and successful New York lawyer. Almost all the things McCartney liked about Eastman rubbed Lennon the wrong way: he was genteel, refined, and of upper-class stock. Klein was a boor next to Eastman, he'd been an orphan, had grown up more or less on the streets, and had had to hustle to make his money. Lennon could relate to this, and persuaded George and Ringo to sign Klein on as their business manager.

On March 21, 1969, Klein announced that he had been appointed business manager for the Beatles under a three-year contract. Klein was to receive 20 percent of all moneys collected by Apple other than under their existing recording contracts, and he would receive 20 percent of any increase he negotiated on those contract figures.

The day before that, John and Yoko made a half-day trip from Paris to Gibraltar, where they were married. "The wedding," John announced, "was quiet and British." They used the publicity of their wedding to hustle attention for their cause, making their honeymoon a week-long "bed-in for peace" in Amsterdam (a stunt "so mystically well-meaning that [it] cost . . . almost nothing and accomplished little more"—Robert Christgau, *Village Voice*).

In the weeks that followed, John officially changed his name from John Winston Lennon to John Ono Lennon and recorded a chronicle of his recent marriage ("Ballad of John and Yoko") with just he and Paul McCartney playing all the instruments and singing.

> Christ, you know it ain't easy
> You know how hard it can be.
> The way things are going
> They're gonna crucify me.
>
> —Lennon/McCartney
> "Ballad of John and Yoko," 1969

"Get Back" and "Don't Let Me Down" had already been released as a single, and the sessions for *Let It Be* had begun. Paul had had the idea to film the sessions and release a movie of the Beatles making an album, but everything was falling apart, and the constant cameras and lights, recording every moment for posterity, only made the problems worse.

It was hell making the film *Let It Be*. When it came out a lot of people complained about Yoko looking miserable in it. But even the biggest Beatle fan couldn't have set through those six weeks of misery. it was the most miserable session on earth.

—John Lennon

Friction came in; business things; relations between us. We were all looking for people in our lives. John had found Yoko; it made things very difficult. He wanted a very intense, intimate life with her; at the same time, we'd always reserved that kind of intimacy for the group.

—Paul McCartney
Musician: Player and Listener

Let It Be was a dismal album (with a few good tracks: John's "Across the Universe" and "Don't Let Me Down," Paul's "Get Back" and "Let It Be"), and it signaled the end of the Beatles. It was obvious to them, if not to the rest of the world. But anyone who heard the album would have figured it out: these four people were no longer happy together, they were bored and peeved and fundamentally uncomfortable with one another, and they needed a long separation, if not a divorce. This is probably why the album was delayed for so long (nearly a year).

Whether out of pride or perseverance, or of nostalgia for the fact that they would probably no longer be together (or out of the hope of some new reconciliation, some new way to exist collectively), they rallied their forces and recorded and released a new album. Just as the colors at sunset are brightest and most intense, so *Abbey Road* was bright and intense, filled with the spark that was missing in *Let It be.*

That fall of 1969, Paul was being declared very dead. Perhaps people realized that the Beatles were finished and, dependent as they were on them, wanted to kill them before they could actually split up, keeping the myth more intact, (kill the bastard before he hurts *us*). But the stories spread (like myth, growing larger with each telling) and the stories grew wilder and wilder: Paul's bare feet on the cover of *Abbey Road* are a sign that he's dead (all the others have shoes on); Paul died a long time ago and that's his brother Michael on the cover (you can tell because Michael's not left-handed); the backward clues on the old records: "I buried Paul," "Turn me on, dead man"; and on and on.

Whatever the reason, all the "Paul is dead" gossip deflected attention from the group's imminent breakup. Lennon, meanwhile, was amazingly active. The Plastic Ono Band (expanded to include Tommy Smothers, Tim Leary, and seemingly anyone who could fit into his and Yoko's Montreal hotel room) recorded Lennon's anthem "Give Peace a Chance." Around the time of *Abbey Road* John had tried to record "Cold Turkey" with the Beatles, but they apparently weren't interested. Lennon recorded the song on his own, with Eric Clapton and the Plastic Ono Band and, with the same lineup, recorded a live album in Toronto. He was finding a lot of new freedom and energy playing with new and different musicians.

That November, Lennon told *Disc and Music Echo:* "I am an artist and my art is peace and I happen to be a musician." In keeping with those ideals, he returned his M.B.E. as a protest against British support of the U.S. in Vietnam, British policy toward Biafra, and his last single, "Cold Turkey," slipping down the charts.

At this point, the Beatles were finished. All that was left was to announce it and let *Let It be* out of the bag.

In *The Beatles: In Their Own Words,* published in England by Omnibus Press, John Lennon described the final breakup:

I said to Paul, "I'm leaving." I knew on the flight over to Toronto: I told Eric Clapton and Klaus that I was leaving then, but that I would probably like to use them as a group. I hadn't decided how to do it—to have a permanent new group or what—then later on, I thought, Fuck, I'm not going to get stuck with another set of people, whoever they are.

I announced it to myself and the people around me on the way to Toronto a few days before. And on the plane I told Allen, "It's over." When I got back, there were a few meetings, and Allen said, "Well, cool it, cool it," there was a lot to do, businesswise you know, and it would not have been suitable at the time.

Then we were discussing something in the office with Paul, and Paul said something or other about the Beatles doing something, and I kept saying "No, no, no," to everything he said. So it came to a point where I had to say something, of course, and Paul said, "What do you mean?"

I said, "I mean the group is over, I'm leaving."

Paul and Allen both said that they were glad that I wasn't going to announce it, that I wasn't going to make an event out of it. I don't know whether Paul said don't tell anybody, but he said, "Oh, that means nothing really happened if you're not going to say anything."

So that's what happened. So, like anybody when you say divorce, their face goes all sorts of colors. It's like he knew really that this was the final thing; and six months later he comes out with whatever. I was a fool not to do it; not to do what Paul did, which was use it to sell a record.

In April 1970, Paul McCartney released his first solo album (one month before the release of *Let It Be*) and announced that he had left the Beatles "because of personal, business, and musical differences."

From there on, it was all lawsuits.

6

THE PLASTIC ONO BAND

Although it was Paul who first announced his split from the Beatles publicly, it was John who actually released the first material that did not include the rest of the Beatles when he put out the controversial *Two Virgins* LP, one of the initial records on the group's newly formed Apple label, in February 1969. Appearing only three months after a much publicized divorce from his first wife, Cynthia, *Two Virgins'* main claim to fame to this day is its cover, a stark black-and-white photograph of John and Yoko in the altogether. When asked the reasons for posing in the nude, especially for such an unflattering portrait—what with John's knobby knees and Yoko's sagging breasts—Lennon expressed the desire to face the public with all his and Yoko's imperfections intact, "just to say we still love each other no matter what."

The album was shunned by record stores and fans alike. When a shop did carry it, *Two Virgins* was packaged in a brown paper bag, which inspired John and Yoko's Bag Production company. Aside from the nude shot of John and Yoko, the cover contains a quote from Paul McCartney; "When two great Saints meet it is a humbling experience." John's desire to let it all hang out found its logical outcome in the album's curious collage of cooing sounds, room noise, and cryptic conversation. Yoko introduced her soon to be influential warbling while John tinkled the ivories on a record every bit as weird now as the first day it came out. In falling in love with Yoko, John began to explore her world of avant-garde art and experimentation, which had always been such an important part of his own work on Beatles tunes as "Strawberry Fields Forever," "Revolution 9," and "I Am the Walrus." Although *Two Virgins* had little commercial value, Yoko's vocal excursions have influenced New Wave Bands from the B-52s to Lene Lovich.

A month after the appearance of *Two Virgins,* and a scant week after McCartney's marriage to photographer Linda Eastman on March 20, John and Yoko were married in Gibraltar.

Amid all this activity, it was remarkable that Lennon was able to continue making records. In May 1969, the newest Apple subsidiary, Zapple Records, released John and Yoko's second collaboration, *Unfinished Music No. 2—Life with the Lions.* Side one consisted of a painful ditty called " 'Cambridge 1969,' " a duet featuring Yoko's characteristic yodeling and John's screeching feedback guitar. Side two was a series of recordings made while the Lennons stayed in a hospital during Yoko's miscarriage. Yoko sang a pair of newspaper stories while John chanted in the background. In one chilling section, there was the sound of the baby's heartbeat, then, silence. John and Yoko were to return to the theme of childbearing in their last record, *Double Fantasy,* but this glimpse into the couple's pain was a little too private to have much impact on the public.

In June, "The Ballad of John and Yoko" came out as a Beatles single, credited to Lennon/McCartney. With Ringo and George unavailable, Paul put aside his personal animosity toward Yoko long enough to overdub bass and drums while John handled both guitar parts. The single not only announced John's undying devotion to Yoko (as opposed to the Beatles, or so many thought) but also continued Lennon's obsession with martyrdom. The hook lyric, "Christ, you know it ain't easy," recalled Lennon's "The Beatles are more popular than Jesus" remark of three years before and caused many radio stations to drop the record from their playlist.

A month later, the theme song for John and Yoko's bed-in, "Give Peace a Chance," was released, and, to thank Paul for his contribution to "Ballad of John and Yoko," John credited the song to Lennon-McCartney, even though he recorded it with the Plastic Ono Band under the sheets in Montreal. This straightforward attempt to write an anthem foreshadowed John's disastrous dalliance with radical politics on *Some Time in New York City,* but, in its own Mother Goose cum mantra way, the tune achieves a moving quality. Indeed, the mourners who gathered outside the Dakota to stand vigil used it as their theme song and it had a stunning impact. With "Give Peace a Chance," John entered a period of intense searching for social and then personal liberation, which was to lead him through primal therapy, Left-wing politics, drugs, and, finally, family. As became customary, the B side contained a Yoko Ono composition, "Remember Love," that showed her until now hidden musical talent.

Fall 1969 saw the release of *Abbey Road,* which included John's "Come Together," yet another Lennon paean to cosmic union and utopian dreams of community. At the same time the infamous *Wedding Album* also came out, the height of the Lennons' self-indulgence. This consisted of a recording made at John and Yoko's wedding, and the album package containing a set of four photo-booth snapshots, a postcard, a picture of a piece of the wedding cake in a white plastic bag, a poster, and a sheaf of hostile press clippings and cartoons. It was a record of the event for everyone who couldn't be there. Side one has Yoko uttering John's name and John uttering Yoko's name ad nauseam. On side two, John and Yoko introduce the aural documentary, a collage of conversations, interviews, and discussions recorded in bed and on the streets of Amsterdam during their honeymoon. At this time John and Yoko became the subject of unrelenting public ridicule and abuse. Yoko was the recipient of numerous death threats for "breaking up the Beatles by putting John under her spell."

Shortly after the appearance of the wedding album, Lennon recorded his first solo composition, a single, "Cold Turkey," later featured on *The Plastic Ono Band—Live Peace in Toronto* album released in December 1969. On the B side, Yoko sings "Don't Worry Kyoko (Mummy's Only Looking for a Hand in the Snow)," an ode to a daughter from a previous marriage who was kidnapped by her legal father and whisked away to some unknown location. The battle for Kyoko was just one example of the legal struggles which had Lennon in and out of court in the seventies. Showing the fatherly concern which led him to give up performing for five years in order to care for his son Sean, Lennon supported Yoko every step of the way in the fight to see her daughter.

"Cold Turkey" is one of Lennon's most underrated songs, a plaintive wail against the horrors of heroin addiction that incorporates Yoko's squawks and squeals into a searing rock-and-roll statement. The album itself was recorded at a rock-and-roll revival in Toronto, featuring John's first live performance since the last Beatles concert back in 1965. Accompanied by Yoko, Eric Clapton, bassist and long-time pal Klaus Voorman, and drummer Alan White, Lennon bashes through a trio of oldies with obvious relish—"Blue Suede Shoes," "Money," and "Dizzy Miss Lizzy"—before tackling "Yer Blues" (from the White Album), "Cold Turkey," and "the reason why we're all here," "Give Peace a Chance." Side two consists of a twenty-minute jam on "Don't Worry Kyoko" that highlights Yoko's painful, caterwauling mother's lament backed by a raucous rock-and-roll accompaniment. Even in this postpunk-rock era. Yoko's unique scat singing sounds horrifically intense.

The dawning of the seventies brought with it the final dissolution of the Beatles. Paul chose to release his own solo *McCartney* album in competition with the Beatles' *Let It Be* that spring, while Lennon continued collaborating with producer Phil Spector on a single,

"Instant Karma." The stark, echoed sound Spector achieved on "Instant Karma" would be Lennon's trademark through his first two solo albums. The sharply defined minimalism of "Instant Karma" struck an immediate chord with the public, and it rose to number one on March 13. One of John's best songs, "Instant Karma" both satirized and summarized Lennon's search for a higher awareness in its hit-bound hook, as an entire generation stood on the threshold of the Me Decade. John's biting wit on the subject foreshadowed the seventies preoccupation with healing a collective psyche torn apart by the turbulent sixties. John was still at the forefront, bravely leading the charge into the post-Beatles, postpeace-and-love era, and "Instant Karma" sounded the clarion call. Written, recorded, and mixed in one day, John once again gave the B side over to Yoko, with "Who Has Seen the Wind?"

Christmas 1970: An album appears in the stores with no title on the cover. Instead, there is a picture of a couple lounging beneath a tree, dreaming the day away. On closer inspection, the couple is revealed to be John and Yoko. The album, *John Lennon Plastic Ono Band,* is considered by most critics to be John Lennon's first solo album. Virtually at the exact same instant, Yoko's sole debut was released, with the same front cover, but it was John's monumental LP which captured all the attention.

Produced with the same stark echo sound Spector achieved on "Instant Karma," *Plastic Ono Band* wiped the slate clean on John's Beatle past to come to grips with the here and now. The album begins with the funereal chiming of bells on "Mother," which deals with John's primal need for the real parents he never had. The lyrics are honed to the bone, simple yet profound. The coda turns into an excruciating primal scream, "Mama don't go/Daddy come home." The entire album expressed Lennon's desperate desire to expiate his innermost fears, while stripping his various personas one by one, until he stood as emotionally naked as he stood physically naked on *Two Virgins*. During this period, John became very involved with

Arthur (*Primal Scream*) Janov's psychological theories, and *Plastic Ono Band* represents Janov's therapeutic techniques being put into practice.

Aside from John and Yoko, who receives album credit for "Wind," the Plastic Ono Band consisted of Ringo Starr and Klaus Voorman at the time. The second song on the album, "Hold On (John)," is a lilting counterpoint to the *Sturm und Drang* of most of the rest of the record, a charming piece of self-advice which urges Lennon to hold on, "it's gonna be alright." The song becomes a paean to the integration of the personality John had seemingly been seeking all his life. "When you're one/Really one/You get things done/Like they never been done." It wasn't the first time, nor would it be the last, that John thought he had attained the wholeness he was searching for.

"I Found Out" is another bitter diatribe against accepted solutions like the counterculture, Christianity, masturbation, Hare Krishna, and drugs. John also takes his first swipe at McCartney in what will become a one-way feud, with Lennon blaming his ex-mate for splitting up the group, even though he knew it had to end. Lennon's answer to the mystery of life? "Can't you do no harm to feel your own pain/I found out." Brutally frank and honest, John tosses off the hippie phenomenon with sarcastic venom. "Don't give me that brother, brother, brother, brother." He also attacks his real parents for abandoning him. "They didn't want me, so they made me a star."

"Working Class Hero" is one of Lennon's most radical songs, but, unlike the later material on *Some Time in New York City,* it employs a double-edged irony which adds to its complexity. Lennon paints a dead-end portrait of a labor force, totally subjugated socially and personally, until there's no way out except submission. But the mournful refrain belies the horror with heroic resolution: "A working class hero is something to be." John comes to grips with the contradiction between his blue-collar roots, his radical socialism, and his vast wealth by weaving a complex catharsis that seeks to break down reality into its various components. He analyzes society's iron-clad control and, by turning the song into sneering sarcasm, urges everyone to take control of his individual destiny. Ten years later, "Working Class Hero" has lost none of its force as a critique of contemporary society. "Isolation" closes out the side and offers a chilling insight into the loneliness at the top. Stung by the media criticism of him and Yoko, John reaches out for understanding, realizing the public will never allow them the luxury of an ordinary life—an ironic prophecy of John's five-year "retirement" which would begin in 1975.

Side two deals with large themes like memory, love, guilt, identity, God, and motherhood. "Remember" is a charming salve from John to Yoko whenever she's feeling blue. "Love" is, likewise, a valentine from Lennon to his wife that tries to define the feeling, only to end up with a series of circular, R. D. Laing equations. "Well Well Well" describs the estrangement between the male and female in nursery rhyme fashion, making explicit the hidden wellspring of alienation inherent in all human relationships. Particularly noteworthy is John's self-guilt, which has always defined his work, from "Help!" to "Watching the Wheels." This is the same guilt which will drive him to support the disintegrating New Left of Abbie Hoffman and Jerry Rubin along with the anarchic street politics of David Peel, a year later.

"Look at Me" deals with everyone's demands and expectations on Lennon, as the singer flounders after a self-image and decides his true nature is defined by the love of another, and his feelings for Yoko.

"God" forms *Plastic Ono Band*'s centerpiece, a ringing disavowal of idols from the *I-Ching* to Elvis, from the Bible to Zimmerman, from the Tarot to Kennedy, and, finally to the Beatles themselves. As John lists the fallen idols one by one, the momentum forces him to confront his own irreducible essence.

The album's coda, "My Mummy's Dead," once more confronts John's pain at the loss of his mother in an automobile accident when he was thirteen. If anything, this is Lennon's "Rosebud," the single event which shaped his entire life—the absence of his real mother and father.

The release of the *Plastic Ono Band* album took the critical world largely by surprise. Never before had an artist presented such a raw and self-indicting confession, harrowing in its stark minimalism. Anyone who dared suggest a reunion of the Beatles was stopped in his tracks by the *Plastic Ono Band*'s denunciatory obituary.

But it wasn't only the revealing psychological themes that made *Plastic Ono Band* the remarkable record it was. As Yoko herself noted about the record, as well as her own solo effort, *Fly*, Lennon's guitar sound was revolutionary on these early Plastic Ono Band LPs.

"If you listen to some of the early records, John is doing some remarkable guitar playing," she said. "Really fantastic sort of avant-garde stuff. His guitar playing was never really appreciated. It shows that kind of mad streak. And I have that, too."

Lennon's twisted guitar playing is shown at its most intense on the B side of the single "Mother," a Yoko Ono track called "Why?" released shortly after the Plastic Ono Band album. That April, John recorded yet another attempt at a political rallying cry, "Power to the People," which was actually pretty provocative for its time, a nervy call to arms that employed every radical chic cliché in the book, though it was quite good fun. The B side was, once again, a Yoko Ono composition, "Touch Me." During the summer of 1971, sandwiched in between Lennon's much bally-hooed interview with *Rolling Stone* and some avant-garde film work with his wife, a single called "God Save Us" came out, written by John and Yoko to earn money for the defense trial of the supposedly obscene magazine *Oz*. "God Save Us" was credited to Bill Elliot and the Elastic Oz Band, while the flip, "Do the Oz," was Elastic Oz Band only. Both sides were penned by Lennon, and it was not the first time John would use a pseudonym to cover up his involvement.

John Lennon, age 9.

An early recording session, 1962, with producer George Martin at left.

Tough punk in Hamburg, Germany, 1961. Stu Sutcliffe lurks in the background.

THE BEATLES

Beatles, wives and friends listen to The Maharishi, 1968.

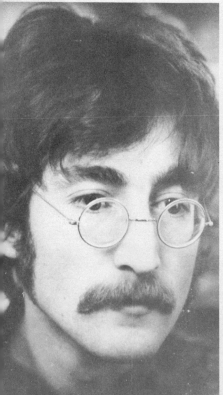

The Beatles and their O.B.E. medals, October 27, 1965.

With first wife Cynthia at the premiere of *How I Won The War*, 1968.

John uncharacteristically with a gun; a film still from Richard Lester's *How I Won The War*, 1968.

One of the last publicity photos taken of The Beatles, 1969.

From the movie ''Magical Mystery Tour.''

Psychedelic pop.

A free lunchtime concert atop the Apple offices in London, 1969.

John and his son Julian, then age 5, at a Rolling Stone concert in December 1968.

John and Yoko cut their hair for peace in 1970, "Year One."

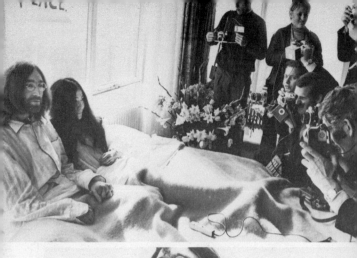

Speaking at a peace rally, 1972.

John and Yoko bed-in for peace the week following their marriage in 1969.

Performing at a 1972 concert benefit for retarded children.

At the Hit Factory to begin recording session for the *Double Fantasy* album. August 1980.

John, Yoko, and their son Sean

Yoko and record producer David Geffen leaving Roosevelt Hospital.

Mourners at a Lennon memorial in Cincinnati.

Julian Lennon and his mother Cynthia.

Ringo Starr and Barbara Bach.

Fans gathered in memoriam outside the archway to the Dakota, December 8, 1980.

London headlines.

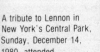

A tribute to Lennon in
New York's Central Park,
Sunday, December 14,
1980, attended
by over 100,000 fans.
Dakota at top right.

Another favorite nom de plume was Dr. Winston O'Boogie, a play on his middle name.

The second album in the Phil Spector-produced trilogy of John Lennon LP's, *Imagine,* appeared in September 1971. While furthering the themes of psychic integration and divestment of the past which characterized *Plastic Ono Band, Imagine* was a more tender, less strident album, in which John turned his attentions away from tearing apart and began the slow process of regeneration. The title track has become one of Lennon's most beloved songs, expressing as it does John's hopes for a utopian future of community, without war, greed, conflict, or hunger. The doleful tune carries within it a feeling of resignation that such a world will always be impossible, and this realization gives "Imagine" its tragic undertone of belief in the face of absurdity.

"Crippled Inside," which features George Harrison on dobro and Nicky Hopkins on piano, among others, expresses Lennon's aversion to the establishment in no uncertain terms. John urges the uptight businessman to shape up, but the song lacks the compassion of, say, Ray Davies, for the white-collar worker as robotic slave. "Jealous Guy" deals with John's fears of losing Yoko, hurting Yoko or making her cry. It is a lovely, touching ode to the moments of insecurity inherent in any relationship and John's admissions reach the listener as shared confidences. "It's So Hard" returns to the sentiments of "Hold On John" though Lennon's pleas for sympathy are beginning to get a little grating by this point. "I Don't Want to Be a Soldier Mama" is the down side of "Give Peace a Chance," a nightmarish chant that sounds like Public Image with Lennon as Johnny Rotten chanting into the maelstrom, "I don't wanna die."

The second side includes some of Lennon's most vituperative, whining bitching, all effectively masked by Spector's orchestral wall of sound. Unlike *Plastic Ono Band, Imagine* is lush and colorful, with a large sound quite unlike the first LP's rigid formalism.

Among the musicians who appear on *Imagine* are

Klaus Voorman, Alan White, Jim Keltner, Mike Pinder, King Curtis, John Barhan, Joey and Tommy Badfinger, as well as Nicky Hopkins and George Harrison. Perhaps significantly, *Imagine* was credited to John Lennon rather than the Plastic Ono Band, with his supporting cast steadily growing in numbers.

"Give Me Some Truth" is typical Lennon; sly, demanding, sarcastic, and bitter, once more on the attack. John's sick and tired of hypocrites, pigheaded politicians, chauvinists, and schizophrenic, egocentric, paranoiac prima donnas. Lines like "No short-haired, yellow-bellied son of tricky dicky is gonna mother hubbard soft-soap me," stands up to the best Lennon lyrics with its angry absurdity. "Oh My Love" is a beautiful love song on the order of the White Album's "Julia," a tribute to the redemptive power of romance.

Of all the songs on *Imagine,* though, none is recalled as often as "How Do You Sleep?" a surprisingly vicious attack on Paul McCartney that is uncharacteristically mean-spirited and one-sided in its vitriol. John went against his own advice by dredging up the bitterness of the Beatles' breakup, and his character assassination does not hold up well. Still, John never said he was any more than human, and subject to the same hostilities and hurts as the rest of us; Paul formed a convenient target. Lennon was not the only one to dismiss McCartney's solo output and domestic lifestyle, though Lennon would eventually find peace in the same family situation he taunted Paul for retreating into.

"How?" is another bit of existential wordplay memorable less for its message than for its dreamy atmosphere and impassioned singing. "Oh Yoko!" is, aside from the title track, the best song on the album. A brilliantly incisive statement on the ubiquity of love, "Oh Yoko!" is John at his most playful, connecting with such irresistible lyrics as "In the middle of a bath, I call your name." There is a touching quality to Lennon's admission of need that transcends his specific situation to touch on the universal.

As John said recently, "The male and the female is better than a male or a female separately, that's what Yoko and I think.

"Being with her makes me free, you know. It makes me whole. I'm a half without her. Male is half without a female."

For her part, Yoko agrees, but she sees things in much more abstract terms, "I believe that love is everything. Everything in the world is really moving because of love. I think, inside of us, we all really believe in it."

That love was channeled into John and Yoko's 1971 yuletide gift, the still potent single, "Happy Xmas (War Is Over)," which was recorded with the Harlem Community Choir. The 45 was pressed in clear green plastic and the flip side is yet another. Yoko cut, "Listen, the Snow is Falling." "Happy Xmas" is one of Phil Spector's most memorable productions, with waves upon waves of sleighbells forming the backdrop to John and Yoko's heartfelt seasonal cheer and wish for worldwide peace.

1972 saw John and Yoko fall under the spell of their adopted home, New York City. The result was the wildly uneven and commercially disastrous *Some Time in New York City* album, released in June. With this LP, John and Yoko plunged headlong into the New York street scene and orthodox radical politics; the result was an album of songs that hewed pretty close to the party line without Lennon's gift for lyrical irony and paradox.

John and Yoko were joined on the album by a New York rock band of little renown called Elephant's Memory, and the overall sound was gut-wrenching r and r, if you managed to ignore the rather too pat sentiments. The first single culled from the disk was the controversial "Woman Is the Nigger of the World," cowritten by John and Yoko about the plight of the female sex. John was attempting to raise his admittedly macho consciousness with such lines as "We make her paint her face and dance/If she won't be a slave, we say that she don't love us . . . While putting her down we pretend that she's above us." Though the sentiments were a little too obvious for many, the politics were correct and the backbeat was strong. For the first time, Yoko herself contributed a trio of solo compositions to a *Plastic Ono Band* LP—"Sisters, O Sisters," "We're All Water," and "Born in a Prison,"—that coexisted with John's own material, a collaboration of equals that would return on *Double Fantasy.*

The album cover was in the form of a newspaper with the various song lyrics appering as headlines and stories. While Lennon attempted to convey that sense of current events, for the most part, *Some Time in New York City* is a dated disappointment.

Yoko still doesn't regret anything about that period. "A lot of things happened. I don't think it was just us. I think that maybe the press blew it up a lot more because it was us. But there were a lot of people doing a lot of things then for the betterment of the world . . . and it worked in a way. I think that the fact that the Vietnam War was stopped at all had a lot to do with the way people resisted it."

John was considerably more chagrined at his involvement. "That radicalism was phony, really, because it was born out of guilt. It was partly that and partly 'cause I'm a chameleon. I always felt guilty that I'd made money, so I had to let people rob me in the disguise of management or whatever. I always felt that I didn't deserve it or there's something wrong with having it. It never made sense to me to have money and think the way I thought. I was always having that turmoil. The radicalism was a combination of having met certain people at certain times. So, I just went along for the trip. You know, what am I doing fighting the American government just so Jerry Rubin can get a decent job?"

Included with the package was an additional live album that was recorded in part at the London Lyceum with the Plastic Ono Band, and at the Fillmore East the previous June with the Mothers of Invention. The London side includes renditions of "Cold Turkey" and "Don't Worry Kyoko" from 1969. The other side took place during a Mothers of Invention concert that was being taped for a live album. Joining Zappa and company for the encore. John and Yoko strolled on-stage unannounced, with Lennon doing a solo spot on guitar, "Baby Please Don't Go," written by one Walter Ward. At this point, the proceedings degenerated into a mad jam listed on the LP as "Jamrag," and Yoko crawled into a large sack with a microphone, wailing away. As a maliciously grinning, demented Zappa egged the crowd into a chant of "Scumbag," Yoko continued writhing in her sack while John blithely strummed away, enjoying the whole thing. The musicians left the stage one by one, leaving Yoko all alone in the bag, screaming at the top of her lungs in the midst of deafening feedback.

It was at this point that John Lennon's world began to unravel. Fighting a deportation order from the United States government for a long forgotten drug conviction and having his relationship with Yoko suddenly on the rocks, it was a wonder he could make any music at all. In November 1973, Lennon released the album *Mind Games,* which revealed a chastened, tentative artist unsure of his next direction. Ditching the politics of *Some Time in New York City, Mind Games* shows John marking time, with embarrassingly little of substance to say. Lennon insisted that, like a great painter, the subject of his work was not as important as the way he expressed himself, but the explanation rang false.

The single from the album, its title track, was the most memorable tune on the LP, a return to the melodicism that was so successful on *Imagine*. And while tracks such as "Bring On the Lucie" and the boogeyin' "Tight A$" are undeniably catchy, they lack the substance of Lennon's most provocative work. One odd tidbit is the "Nutopian International Anthem," three seconds of dead air which harken back to John and Yoko's avant-garde heyday in '69.

Shortly after the appearance of *Mind Games,* John and Yoko split up, she remaining in New York, he traveling, eventually landing in Los Angeles.

Lennon's year there was one long orgy of drink and drugs, highlighted by John getting thrown out of the Troubadour for heckling the Smothers Brothers and wearing a Kotex taped to his face, among other mischief. Still, despite his emotional turbulence, John collaborated on a few projects with other musicians. He dueted with good friend Elton John on a live version of his own "Lucy in the Sky with Diamonds" as well as an original Lennon composition, "One Day at a Time." The credit read, reggae guitars courtesy of Dr. Winston O'Boogie. John also appears on the B side of Elton's "Philadelphia Freedom" single, a live version of "I Saw Her Standing There." Lennon even appeared onstage with Elton to perform "Lucy in the Sky." John also contributed two songs on David Bowie's *Young Americans* LP, including his own "Across the Universe" and "Fame," in which he shares a cowriting credit with Bowie and guitarist Carlos Alomar, and sings.

As mentioned above, Lennon produced Harry Nilsson's *Pussycats* album, a hilariously irreverent romp which perfectly matched this wacky duo's caustic sensibilities. John's touch is obvious on the album, giving Nilsson the heavily echoed production Spector gave Lennon on his solo LPs. Nilsson rasps his way through covers of "Many Rivers to Cross," "Subterranean Homesick Blues," "Save the Last Dance for Me," and "Rock Around the Clock," and you can practically hear John chortling in the background. The liner notes contain the quote, "Everything is the opposite of what it is" (Dr. Winston O'Boogie, M.D. Manic Depressive). As he admitted, Lennon was reaching the end of his tether.

But John forced himself to quit drinking and began the first, tentative steps toward reconciling with Yoko. His partnership with Elton John resulted in the single "Whatever Gets You Through the Night," released in September 1974 to coincide with John's new album, *Walls and Bridges*. Featuring as its cover a drawing done by John when he was eleven years old, *Walls and Bridges* represented a slight comeback from the desultory *Mind Games,* though it still grappled with the meaninglessness and depression brought on by Lennon's separation from Yoko. "Going Down on Love" is a song of remorse for a busted relationship, its lyrics an apologetic plea almost too personal to share. John's desperation is as real here as it was on his first solo album, though the mood is once again, pessimistic rather than hopeful. Bobby Keys's tenor sax gives the tune its distinctive texture, while Elton John sits in on organ, piano, and vocal harmonies.

"What You Got" echoes the self-help therapy of "Hold On John," even as it mourns Lennon's breakup with Yoko. "Bless You" continues the obsession with Yoko, praying for the reconciliation which was apparently at hand. "Sacred" takes Lennon back to the emotional vulnerability of "Help!" and "I'm So Tired," with its vision of existential malaise.

The second single from *Walls and Bridges,* "No. 9 Dream," leads off side two. In the mold of "Imagine," "No. 9 Dream" is a vision of togetherness that evokes a space beyond music and maya, transcending the material world. It is one of John's loveliest melodies, an aching cry for love that evokes the ephemeral in its attempt to touch the eternal. How could Yoko possibly resist such a noble request for forgiveness? "Surprise, Surprise (Sweet Bird of Paradox)" is an ode to sexual pleasure and very possibly about May Pang, the oriental woman John was hanging around with during this time. "Steel and Glass" returns to the turf of "Nowhere Man" and "Crippled Inside," to perhaps lash out at an El Lay music-bizzer. "Beef Jerky" is one of the only Lennon instrumentals ever recorded while "Nobody Loves You (When You're Down and Out)" is John again feeling sorry for himself. "Ya Ya" is a throwaway version of the old Lee Dorsey chestnut, notable mainly for the presence of John's first son by Cynthia, Julian, on drums.

Yoko responded to John's overtures and the two were reunited in New York. Even she admitted it was hard to stop loving John. "During those eighteen months, part of us was always communicating. We were both sort of exploring. At the same time, John would call me and complain about what was happening to him. We never completely lost touch." John immediately began working on his long-delayed "oldies" project with Phil Spector. Lennon had first laid down tracks for the LP in 1973, but they sat in a vault for almost a year and a half before John turned to them again. This time, with the security of being reunited with Yoko, John set about recording the album that was to be called *Rock 'n' Roll* with a revitalized urgency.

1975 was a very good year for John. His *Rock 'n' Roll* album proved to be an acclaimed revival of some of Lennon's jukebox favorites, a chance for John to forget about messages and rock out like his idols, Elvis Presley and Chuck Berry. Along the way, there were delightful surprises, like Lennon's version of Berry's "You Can't Catch Me," which sounds exactly like "Come Together," probably intentionally. The single from the album, and the last one John would release for five years, or until "Starting Over," was a touching rendition of "Stand By Me." The flip side even contains a Lennon original, "Move Over Ms. L," an upbeat raver that showed John in rare form. Five years after the Beatles urged us to "get back," here was Lennon, swiveling his hips to standards like "Ready Teddy," "Do You Want to Dance," and "Sweet Little Sixteen."

Meanwhile, John celebrated the birth of a son, Sean, on October 9 (his own birthday) by winning his battle to remain in the States. That same month, a compilation album of the Plastic Ono Band's "greatest hits," *Shaved Fish,* came out, including such tracks as the singles "Give Peace a Chance," "Power to the People," "Instant Karma," and "Happy Xmas (War Is Over)." The LP jacket contains a prophetic liner note: "A conspiracy of silence speaks louder than words"—Dr. Winston O'Boogie. John was preparing to withdraw from the public eye and spend time with his wife and new son.

During the summer of 1980, though, just as suddenly as he had disappeared, John Lennon and Yoko Ono emerged. Rumors flew that the pair were entering the Record Plant to work on a new album. They contacted producer Jack Douglas, who had engineered the *Imagine* and *Some Time in New York City* albums along with a bunch of unreleased Yoko solo albums, to put together a band for their new material. They chose the thirty-five-year-old Bronx native mainly because he was one of the few engineers who had a rapport in the studio with Yoko. "The rest of them used to laugh or hold their ears when Yoko was recording her material," said Douglas. "But, with my background in the opera and avant-garde, I could appreciate what she was trying to do."

After a brief sojourn to Bermuda, where the two wrote the songs which eventually became *Double Fantasy*, John and Yoko returned to New York and entered the Record Plant. Douglas said of Lennon's last work:

We recorded the material one for one. One of John's songs, followed by one of Yoko's. We cut twenty-two tunes in all. John came in loaded with energy. Yoko wasn't quite sure how her stuff was coming out at first, and then, the second week, when we got to her better material, she started to really groove and become confident about the direction of the recording. Yoko's songs have sort of a New Wave, dance-type sound.

To me the record is like "The Ballad of John and Yoko and Sean." I think John wanted to come back onto the scene as the great tunesmith he is. The songs run the gamut from thirties- and forties-styled orchestrations to gospel. The songs that are in the can are more experimental and not quite as commercial as the ones on *Double Fantasy*. This record features a group of songs which are accessible to a really wide market. John wants to reach out to the most people possible. He feels these songs address the concerns of his own peer group, his age group. Yoko is more likely to reach the younger kids with her sound.

Indeed, the initial impression one has upon hearing the first single from *Double Fantasy,* John's "Staring Over" backed with Yoko's "Kiss Kiss Kiss," is that Yoko's song is much more au courant, much more exciting, much more with-it than John's rather maudlin, though catchy love song. It is, of course, impossible to listen to John's homilies about love and family now without feeling remorse over his senseless death. The man who was never afraid to share his fears and foibles with the rest of us finally seemed happy and fulfilled—and who are we to begrudge him that?

On *Double Fantasy,* John's reliance on Yoko was more apparent than ever. On "Starting Over," John succeeds in reaffirming his love for Yoko while at the same time using the song as a metaphor for his reentrance of the music business. The tune has gained an eerie resonance from John's untimely demise. "Clean-up Time" sings of the joys of making bread, while "Watching the Wheels" is classic Lennon, about the sheer pleasure of daydreaming for daydreaming's sake. "Woman" and "Dear Yoko" are highly personal love letters, redeemed by John's vulnerable delivery.

It is Yoko's dance tunes, though, that make *Double Fantasy* come alive, and how ironic is that? Final achieving the recognition as an artist which was long overdue her, Yoko's critical acclaim delighted John, who was assembling tracks for an Ono solo album the night of his death. An unreleased cut from that album, "Walking on Thin Ice," is a masterpiece, with Yoko's seagull shrieks finding their emotional resonance in a modernistic rock-and-roll framework. As Yoko's star began to rise, John looked to the future with all the more enthusiasm.

7

TWO VIRGINS: THE EXCLUSIVE NEWSWEEK INTERVIEW

"The dream is over," he had reminded us. "I gotta get down to reality." And so in 1975, upon the birth of his son, Sean, and the end of his four-year fight with the Immigration Service to remain in the United States, John Ono Lennon disappeared from public view.

The "dream," of course was the Beatles—and despite his seclusion, the myth lived on. Lennon was rumored to be moping about the twenty-eight rooms in his five Dakota condominium apartments, listening to old Beatles records and watching his hair turn gray. One newspaper report spotted him at a rock club with two bodyguards, "protecting his reputation"—a journalese aside for saying his arrogance was showing. Another found something bucolic brewing in Virginia, and suggested that Lennon had turned cow farmer. Was the erratic artist working up a new sound?

Beatlemaniacs never die—they just grow up to be rock writers. With a little help from their friend, photographer Bob Gruen, I located the Lost Beatle and his wife at the Hit Factory, where they were excitedly recording *Double Fantasy,* their first collaborative album in eight years. On the eve of his fortieth birthday, Lennon was ready to step out of the shadows. First, I'd meet Yoko. Beneath the Mona Lisa veneer—the inscrutable smile, the flawless skin, the whisper-shy voice

—she's about as frail as Darth Vader. David Geffen, president of Geffen Records, their label, recalls the first time she summoned him from Los Angeles. "I was at her [Dakota] office at 9:00 a.m.," he relates. "There she was, in a white chair, all in black, sunglasses, Sherman cigarettes, the whole thing. She said, 'Yes? What do you want?' I didn't know how to respond—I thought *she* wanted something. So I said, 'I'd like to release your records.' She said, 'Of course you would. Who wouldn't? We know who you are, and we decided to make a deal with you.' "

She hadn't yet asked for his birthdate and address to chart his numbers. That would come later. But they came up lucky, and so did mine. Three days later, I found myself shoulder to shoulder at the Hit factory console with popdom's most perplexing pair, while they cooed and cajoled and wrestled their way through songs of love, of fear, of anger and reconciliation. Yoko bashfully reminded me that in the old days at London's Apple Studios, engineers would scatter like straws in the wind when she started singing. "I'd say, 'hey, Where are you going?' " she laughed. Not so this time around. "We're like spiritual advisers," Lennon told me. "I don't want to sing if she's not there, and vice versa. It's like a play—we wrote it and we're acting in it. It's John and Yoko—you can take it or leave it . . . otherwise [laughing], it's cows and cheese, my dear!"

Pale and whippet-thin on his macrobiotic diet, Lennon had finally lost the Beatle baby fat—those years of "steak and potatoes, whiskey and Coke." But he hadn't lost his talent for whimsy and wordplay, despite five years as a self-described househusband. In the old Liverpool lilt, he had ushered me into the studio, extending a plate of sushi and the greeting, "Hi! I'm Howard Garbo—or is it Greta Hughes, today, mother?" he said, with a gentle swipe at Yoko. The most imposing thing about him? That bent nose, which still drooped from the Restoration face like a wax Cyrano!

Whether we were munching eel, sipping "Zen blended" coffee on West 57th Street, or limousining our way uptown, Lennon seemed eager to talk, self-assured and secure in his newly settled life. Until the subject of the Beatles came up. He insisted that he didn't need the chemistry of that magical collaboration to produce great songs. " 'The good old days' is garbage. Let's dig up Glenn Miller," he shot back. "I'm not against collaborating with other people—I'm not looking to play all the instruments. But I'm not looking to go back to school, and going back to the Beatles is like going back to school." Still, Lennon refused to completely rule out the possibility of such an occurrence. "None of us want to be the first to say never," he sighed. "Never is such a long time. . . . It's been five years since I've recorded. It could have been twenty. Life is long—and I've got another forty or fifty years to keep doing this. Age is irrelevant to self-expression."

BARB: Why did you virtually disappear from public view for five years?

JOHN: Because I'll be forty and Sean will be five and I wanted to give five solid years of being there all the time. I hadn't seen my first son, Julian, grow up, and now there's a seventeen-year-old man on the phone talking about motorbikes. I was not there for his childhood at all. I was on tour. And *my* childhood was something else. I don't know what price one has to pay, I don't know how the game works, but there's a price to pay for inattention of children. And if I don't give him attention from zero to five, then I'm damn well gonna have to give it from sixteen to twenty because it's owed, it's like the law of the universe. There's no way—they're gonna get that attention somehow or other.

BARB: How did you begin to shape your days?

JOHN: Just like any housewife. My life was built around Sean's meals. Six o'clock I get up, have a cup of tea, no caffeine, and plan what Sean's going to have for breakfast, work out what he had the day before. He comes out 7:38, we communicate, have breakfast, 10:00. He's either gone somewhere or going somewhere to do something, and then I'm thinking about the next meal. Like Mrs. Higgins in Wisconsin.

BARB: Was yours a decision to withdraw from music making itself, or from all the ancillary pressures of being John Lennon—the lawsuits, the immigration problems, etc.?

JOHN: A bit of both. You see I'd been under contract since I was twenty-two and I was always *supposed* to, *supposed* to. I was *supposed* to write a hundred songs by Friday, *supposed* to have a single out by Saturday, *supposed* to do this and do that. It dawned on me that the reason I became an artist was freedom; because I couldn't fit into the classroom, the college, the society, I was the outsider. And that freedom was what I cherished—that was the plus for all the minuses of being an oddball . . . that I was free, and everybody else had to go to the office. But suddenly, it was exactly the opposite of what I had set out to be. I was obliged to a record company, obliged to the media, obliged to the public, obliged to the American immigration, obliged to go to court every time some asshole bumped into me on the street.

So I said, "What the hell is this? I'm not free at all." I know freedom is in the mind but I couldn't clear my mind. So it was time to regroup.

The fear in the music business is that you don't exist if you're not in the gossip columns, or on the charts, at Xenon with Mick Jagger or Andy Warhol. I just wanted to remember that I existed at all.

At first it was very hard not to be doing something musical because I felt I ought to be. But musically my mind was just a big clutter. It wasn't a question of not having anything to say—if you listen to my early records, there's a dumb song on *Sgt. Pepper* called "Good Morning." There's absolutely nothing to say— just descriptions of paintings of what is. I never have illusions about having something to say but, "It's OK, good morning, good morning, good morning," as the dumb song goes. Quack, quack, quack. It wasn't a matter of nothing to say—it was a matter of no clarity and no desire to do it BECAUSE I WAS SUPPOSED TO. There was a hard withdrawal period, what people must go through at sixty-five, and then I started being a househusband, and swung my attention onto Sean. Then I realized, I'm not supposed to be doing something—I *am* doing something. And then I was free.

BARB: Did you just stop listening to music?

JOHN: I listened mostly to classical music or to Muzak. I'm not interested in other people's work, only so much as it affects me. I have the great honor of never having been to Studio 54, and I've never been to any rock clubs. The *Soho News* said I went to see Jerry Lee Lewis at the Ritz. I was never even there. It's funny how an artist's image exists independently of one. It just carried on living. It was going to clubs and being written about, and I wasn't even there!

BARB: You didn't feel you were missing something?

JOHN (*snappishly*): It's like asking Picasso, has he been to the museum lately? Picasso didn't go to the museums. He was either painting or eating or fucking. Picasso lived where he lived and people came to see *him*. That's what I did. Did Picasso go down to some studio and watch somebody paint? I don't want to see other people paint. I'm just not interested in other people's work—only as much as it affects me. If it's on the news and someone said "This is the latest punk guy and he's just killed himself," of course I know about Sid Vicious. I pick it up the same as you—from the TV and *Newsweek*. But I don't go down to clubs to listen. The only person I ever went to see in London during the swing sixties era was Jimi Hendrix and Bob Dylan at the Isle of Wight . . . the summer of peace and love. I was too busy *doing* it to be watching other people. The competition doesn't interest me unless it's really phenomenal, and then it will be around longer than one night in a club. All the performers I ever saw, from Little Richard to Jerry Lee Lewis, I was always disappointed. I preferred the record.

GETTING FREE

BARB: Yoko was talking about the concept of 'Maleness.' She told me that in your earlier days when everybody thought that John and Yoko were so happy together, there was a lot of feuding and bickering, mostly about your macho tendencies. Have you come a long way from the guy who wrote at age twenty-three that "women should be obscene and not heard"?

JOHN: I was a working-class macho guy that didn't know any better. Yoko taught me about women. I was used to being served, like Elvis and a lot of the stars were. And Yoko didn't buy that. She didn't give a shit about Beatles—what the fuck are the Beatles? I'm Yoko Ono! Treat me as me." That was the battle. She came out with "Woman Is the Nigger of the World" in 1968 as the title of an article she wrote for *Nova* magazine. Because things were like they were, I took the title and wrote the song.

But it was her statement and what she was saying to the world she was saying to Lennon in spades. I had never considered it before. From the day I met her, she demanded equal time, equal space, equal rights. I didn't know what she was talking about. I said, "What do you want, a contract? You can have whatever you want, but don't expect anything from me or for me to change in any way. Don't impinge in my space." "Well," she said, "The answer to that is I can't be here. Because there is no space where you are. Everything revolves around you. And I can't breathe in that atmosphere. I'm an artist, I'm not some female you picked up backstage." Well, I found out. And I'm thankful to her for the education.

I was used to a situation where the newspaper was there for me to read, and after I'd read it, somebody else could have it. It didn't occur to me that somebody else might want to look at it first. I think that's what kills people like Presley and others of that ilk. So-called stars who die in public and lots of people who die privately. The king is always killed by his courtiers, not by his enemies. The king is overfed, overdrugged, overindulged, anything to keep the king tied to his throne. Most people in that position never wake up. They either die mentally or physically or both. And what Yoko did for me, apart from liberating me to be a feminist, was to liberate me from that situation. And that's how the Beatles ended. Not because Yoko split the Beatles, but because she showed me what it was to *be* Elvis Beatle and to be surrounded by sycophants and slaves who were only interested in keeping the situation as it was. And that's a kind of death.

She said to me, "You've got no clothes on." Nobody had dared tell me that before. Nobody dared tell Elvis Presley that, and I doubt if anybody ever dared to tell Mick Jagger, Paul McCartney, or Bob Dylan that they had no clothes on. I didn't accept it at first. "But I *am* clothed! Everything is perfect—*you're* crazy. Nobody tells me—I'm God. I'm King John of England. Nobody tells me nuthin'." Because nobody had. She told me, "You absolutely have no clothes on, and that man whisperin' in your ear is Machiavelli." "But he's been with me for twenty years!" "Then he's been screwin' you for twenty years." "Really?" I couldn't face any of that. She still tells me the truth. It's still painful.

BARB: And did you then have to withdraw from the Beatles?

JOHN: I was always waiting for a reason to get out of the Beatles from the day I made *How I Won the War* in 1966. I just didn't have the guts to do it, you see. Because I didn't know where to go. I remember why I made the movie. I did it because the Beatles had stopped touring and I didn't know what to do. So instead of going home, and being with the family, I immediately went to Spain with Dick Lester because I couldn't deal with not being continually onstage. That was the first time I thought, My God, what do you do if this isn't going on? What is there? There's no life without it.

And that's when the seed was planted that I had to somehow get out of this, without being thrown out by the others. But I could never step out of the palace because it was too frightening.

BARB: Didn't the other Beatles realize that, too?

JOHN: You can *believe* the others never thought of it. That's why they're still in a state of shock. Paul has carried on doing it. He never stopped one day.

BARB: Now, Yoko, what attracted you to John?

YOKO: It was just an instinct, I think. I went to London from New York, and I met all these English men. And most of them were . . . sort of, very feminine, you know? And I thought, oh, is it going to be all like this? And then there was this guy who looked like a guy and we understood each other. He has a very intelligent side that appealed to me, and also a kind of sensitivity. I thought, He understands me. That's sort of rare. Most men really don't.

BARB: Yoko said you read *The First Sex* [by Elizabeth Gould Davis]. Do you think male fantasies and female fantasies are that different?

JOHN: No, not really. *The First Sex* has not much to do with sex, it's archaeology and all that. It made me cry, that book. Because I saw myself in there. As an individual male and representing all males. To get upset about the Holocaust and slavery is one thing, but to understand woman, her situation, is overwhelming. And that's why it'll be a long, hard fight. It's more than just releasing slaves from 200-year slavery. Or Jews from a 2000-year attack. Or the Irish from 1000-year domination. It's more cosmic than that. When I read the book, it overwhelmed me.

BARB: Yoko thought that one of the reasons you took such responsibility with Sean was in a kind of atonement . . .

JOHN: Probably. If I can't deal with a child, I can't deal with anything. No matter what artistic gains I get, or how many gold records, if I can't make a success out of my relationship with the people I supposedly love, then everything else is bullshit.

CREATIVITY

JOHN: I used to go through hell thinking I don't own any of my songs, and then it dawned on me that I never owned them in the first place.

BARB: Do you remember what you said—you said that "We created—Paul and I created it," so that that *is* the concept of ownership. . . .

JOHN: Well, Paul and I were the channels . . . you have to be in tune. It's like when you talk about God, you know, I say "God," I mean "God," I mean "Goddess," I mean "It." I have to remember that everything I say has more meaning when it's printed, right? But when I refer to God in private, I don't have to go "God," "Gods," "Goddesses, "It," you know, like, Yoko, or whoever I'm talking to, understands that I'm talking about "It" more than One Old Man in the Sky . . . I can't keep up with myself, you know, I'm not used to hearing myself played back, for a long time— but you caught me out there, it's just a matter of semantics.

BARB: Okay. But I did want to ask you about the idea of it being a gift kind of borrowing the whole notion of eastern thought—and, are you Buddhists?

JOHN: No. No, I'm nothing. No, no, no label. You can call me a Zen Christian, a Zen Pagan. A Zen Marxist. Yoko's nothing—I like labels! You know, pick it—I don't belong to anything.

BARB: Okay. But there might have been philosophers, people who influenced you—obviously—

JOHN: I read a lot of so-called stuff, but the acknowledgement or rediscovery that I'd have known it in the first place, was the release I got from suffering from having though I'd lost something I never owned in the first place. I don't own the copyright to anything I wrote up until *Walls and Bridges*. So I don't own any of the old so-called Beatles songs. I get writer royalties from them, but I don't own the copyright. I have to ask permission to do things to it, or whatever, and that used to make me suffer, and think I'd been robbed and ripped . . .

BARB: But that's not the same thing as having

influences, along the way and guideposts or philosophy
—I mean, it's possible to absorb the substance of
somebody without absorbing the material. . . .

JOHN: Oh sure, sure, but what I'm saying is it has
to be a self-realization. I might have read that somewhere, that people don't own music, and I read it a
hundred times, but it didn't make sense to me until it
dawned on me that I'd have known it myself, you
know what I mean? So it's like I was saying to somebody—it's like some of the parables—Christ's parables
—some of them are only making sense to me now,
after a whole life of sitting in church or school and
listening to that, moany moany moany, it was just
moany moany moany for years, and then I hear it
again sometime, and I think: God—that's what he
means. The one that stopped me last year some time,
was the parable of the ten talents. Where they took
the—they give him all ten and went away, and one
buried it and one kept it, and one trebled it, then when
he got back, the guy took it off the one who'd kept
hold of it, and that made sense to me, suddenly.

YOKO: It's very good that there's no ownership,
that's very basic and fundamental, just as water, or
life, or air, all the most fundamental things are free.
And shared by everybody. An idea, it sounds like that
too. And when a song is close to a natural idea, then it
becomes something that circulates, without a concept
of ownership.

JOHN: Because you can't own—how can you
own it? It's insane. I can't believe that I would think
that I owned it before—that's what's so strange.

BARB: But that is really how we all are, I mean
here . . . in the record industry. . . .

YOKO: Yeah, but the fact that we can share
means that there's something to share.

JOHN: It's an illusion—ownership is an illusion.
Like possession. Ownership is the same as possession.
It's impossible.

BARB: I know. But tell that to someone who's
eighteen years old, and they'll say—

JOHN: Ah, well I'm not eighteen, I'm forty, well

they have to find out for themselves. But you know, that's what getting older means. Understanding what things really are.

BARB: I don't think that anyone expects that Yoko and John will have the same impact as the Beatles.

JOHN: Well, who's expecting that?

BARB: That's what I'm asking you. Do you think you can have a solid, respectable sensibility or as a duo . . .

JOHN: We don't even think about . . .

YOKO: We don't compare it with the Beatles. . . .

BARB: No, not to be compared with;

YOKO: But you brought it up! You've compared us!

JOHN: Anybody that compares John and Yoko with, you know, four guys, is already on the wrong tack, so we can drop them from the club already, right? Compare it with Fred and Ginger or Les Paul and Mary—and comparisons are odious anyway. You see, the same thing people asked the Beatles—you know "What do you think bout so-and-so?"—we're making it for ourselves. And so the concentration now is on the record.

BARB: No expectations?

JOHN: Expectations that it will be understood and accepted for what it is, when we've made it, but we ain't made it yet, so how can we have expectations?

YOKO: They compared the Beatles with Elvis, you know, Elvis is a man who had a good voice and all that. . . .

BARB: When you have hindsight, nobody—I mean, there's not an expectation—that it would be *this*, but I'm asking you what's really the nature of what you would like it to be?

YOKO: Well, you know it could be, you know what we are . . .

JOHN: Whatever it is!

YOKO: Whatever it is. But what *we* are—we never think in terms of "Well, will we have the same respectability" and this and that—first of all, I don't think "respectability" is a nice word—to use—a nice adjective for people.

JOHN: The Beatles were abhorred. And *then* called respectable.

BARB: How about, how about the word "impact"?

JOHN: If you think we're looking to be the Beatles, we're not—I don't know what you mean—

BARB: No, no . . .

JOHN: Asking Paul that, who has four guys and a group, you know, almost the same lineup, is more relevant—but that's irrelevant too. . . . Wings are Wings and Beatles are Beatles and John and Yoko is John and Yoko.

BARB: Then I—I'd really like to phrase it simply as—what do you think your impact can be? What would you like it to be?

JOHN: There's John and Yoko and they present this—thing—and you can take it or leave it. Otherwise, it's cows and cheese, my dear!! It's for US, and all the people that want something from us, you know.

YOKO: You can't really think about any impact, or any, you know, any reaction . . .

JOHN: If you thought about that, you couldn't do anything. In fact, you know when I was just singing then—the point where it always goes out of key, off tune, or out of phrasing, or whatever it is, is the point when you're thinking. *Not* thinking is the only way to get it right. To play music, to sing, to paint. Like the Zen painters paint. They train for all those times and make that one stroke. So for us to even presuppose what somebody's going to suppose is supposed, while we're still painting, is impossible—because we couldn't do it. And its impact will be whatever its impact will be when IT hits the airwaves. And then we can see— "Oh, oh I hope it, oh—I wonder if it" and we can watch it, reacting, then we can watch it.

YOKO: Because you know, there's that parable about, you know, an eight-legged monster walking very smoothly, and—probably it's a reporter!—you know somebody asks, "Well, how do you manage to walk so beautifully with eight legs?" and so the monster stops and thinks, and says, "Well, I put this leg forward, and then—this—and then, you know, that," and he couldn't walk anymore. You know, so we refuse to think about that. We are what we are and we are giving what we are.

BARB: Is there a difference between the nature of Lennon, solo artist, and Yoko, solo artist, and what you're doing now?

YOKO: The sum is larger than the . . . no, no, what is that . . .

JOHN: Yeah, yeah it is that—the male and the female is better than a male, or a female, separately— that's what we think.

BARB: No, I'm talking about the content of what you're doing.

JOHN: The content is the result of us being together. So. Because that's just what it is. It's a result of us being together. That's what the content is. So I mean, one couldn't stand in the background and present the whole idea, and you know, she could get another guy to do the male part, or I could get another girl to do the female part—that would be crazy wouldn't it? So it's like, we wrote the play and we're acting in it. So that's what the content *is*.

BARB: Does working with Yoko free you to do something that you could not do?

JOHN: Oh, sure . . . I don't know what it is, but it's . . . but BEING with Yoko makes me free, you know. Being with Yoko makes me whole, you know, I'm a half without her. Male is half without a female.

BARB: Do you have weaknesses? Do you see strengths and weaknesses as collaborators?

YOKO: Well, together we're very strong. And this time around, for some reason, we haven't really found it to be a weak collaboration at all really.

JOHN: Yeah, this time was easier than the first time. Because the first time I was still carrying a lot of Beatles stuff in my head and on my back.

BARB: I want to go back to the question of strengths and weaknesses. Can you look at that and say, "this is a problem," I mean . . .

JOHN: Oh yes! I mean, that's why—the thing is, if I see, if she's there, she's the only one that can really tell if I'm doing it right or not. Jack can tell if I'm doing it on pitch, or if I'm doing it correct. But she can tell if my spirit is good. And I don't want to sing if she's not there. That's what she does.

YOKO: Generally—Jack can tell my voice— what to do et cetera, but I mean, John is there to check the spirit for it, you know. And it's very nice.

JOHN: We're like spiritual advisers to each other. You can do it correct, but there's something not there, only somebody close to each other, like this can tell each other what it is. But the spirit is in the way it's being performed.

BARB: It's been five years—in five years there have been different roles that you have pursued in the marriage—the relationship . . .

JOHN: Well, look, you tell us. You're going to have to judge when it's finished, and then call us and say that you saw a difference, because now we're just in it, like craft, and just knitting and doing it, and I can't get that concept feeling about it—maybe there's all sorts in there that we don't even know yet, you know?

YOKO: Yeah, we're speechless about it. You know, we're like a dancer, who's on stage, and doing this movement. And then you say, "How does it look to you?" I'm not looking at it, I'm dancing!

BARB: Why did you leave Yoko in 1973?

JOHN: The truth about the separation was she kicked *me* out . . . so I (*laughter*) was adrift at sea . . . and there was nobody to protect me from myself, which is fine. I should be able to look after myself but I never had, and there was Epstein or Paul to cover up for me. I'm not putting Paul down and I'm not putting Brian down. They'd done a good job in containing my personality from not causing too much trouble.

BARB: Why did Yoko put you out?

JOHN: I was being an animal, and not considerate and she rightly thought, 'If that's the way you want to be, then not here with me'. So there I was, floating around.

BARB: Tell me what happened when you went out to Los Angeles in 1973.

JOHN (*with mock horror*): My "lost weekend"? It lasted for eighteen months. I was like an elephant in a zoo, aware that it's trapped but not able to get out. It's an extension of the craziness that I'd been doing with the Beatles in Hamburg or Liverpool, but it had been covered up by the people surrounding us. So when I freaked out, there would be Paul or Epstein to say, "What he *really* means is he's just a normal boy from a normal family who likes to shear sheep." And the machinery around us would take care of the business. By the time we got to America, we were old hands at it. But if you look back at the Beatles' first national press coverage, it was because I sent a guy to the hospital for calling me a fag, saying I slept with Brian Epstein.

BARB: I remember reading something, I thought it was kind of touching, when you said you saw her backstage at the Elton John concert [in 1975] and you didn't know whether to approach her, you felt very nervous . . .

JOHN: Yeah, terrified, yeah . . .

BARB: Did you want to come back to her?

JOHN: Oh sure, I'd been calling on the phone, and she said no . . . no, no, no. So I found myself involved making Harry Nilsson records, which I should never have got involved in, and had all the musicians living with me in the house, and it was just a big madhouse, and I realized that I was in charge. I wasn't just one of the boys—in fact the bills were going to be coming to me and that a company, I can't remember who the hell it was, would be expecting me to produce this record out of this gang of drunken lunatics, Keith Moon, Harry, me, all these people—so I just quit drinking like that and quit everything, and then I became Him to the rest of the guys, suddenly I was Him . . .

BARB: Right, the manager, the boss . . .

JOHN: Yeah, the one that wasn't lying on the floor, so there was a bit of that goin' on . . . But that's when I sort of woke up, still very fuzzy, because I'd been drinking like a lunatic, and it takes it out of your body. And so then I finished what I could of the work in L.A. and dragged it back to New York. Even though she said that I couldn't come back, I had to get back to New York anyway, and get rid of Harry (*laughter*) and this business, and then see where I'm at. So the first instinct was to stop drinking and playing around with the guys and the thing was to finish off the responsibilities I had, which was my own album, and Harry Nilsson's album, which was very difficult because everybody else was still loony. And I did that, and then, I don't know how long it took before she said, "Okay, come and see me," and then we never looked back (*laughter*) . . . and then it was all right.

BARB: What year was that?

JOHN: Well, I'm not good at dates, but whatever it was, it's all documented. That's why I don't have to bother with dates . . . because it's on paper in the files somewhere. Right?

BARB: Did that incident make you realize that you also had to spend more time together?

JOHN: It made me realize a long time before that . . . uh . . . what I'd lost was a whole life with somebody and that even though I don't think there are many Yokos around, in the world, that even the possibility of meeting somebody of that ilk, that I could deal with on an intelligent level as well as man and woman that one . . . it's the old game of everybody's divorcing, you know? . . . but what they forget is that you have to start again and you go through the same pattern with the next person anyway, and you reach the same points, then if you can't go through those points, then that's when they divorce again. And you go through the first romantic thing and the farce and you go through the this-and-the-that and you go through the whole damn thing again. And that even presuming that I could ever get involved with some other woman who could involve me totally like her, and the chance of that would be very rare . . . nine years later I'd be in the same place and face the same situation and make the same decision again. I do a lot of dumb things, but I'm not stupid.

BARB: Do you have any regrets about the last five years?

JOHN: No, none.

BARB: Do you think it's possible to spend too much time with a child?

JOHN: No, not for a child—that's all grown-up garbage . . . excuses for not being a child. In all the native cultures, the children don't leave the mother's back until two, and they certainly don't leave the environment until they want. A child will naturally leave you when it's ready.

BARB: Do you think part of that came from the fact that you had been abandoned?

JOHN (*laughs*): No, no, otherwise I would have been the same with Julian. Part of it came from the fact that it was so-called love child, whatever that expression is, and I was a more grown-up person when I had Sean than when I had Julian at twenty-three. I had Julian at the beginning before the Beatles made it, just when we were still in Liverpool. I was just a young kid. So I didn't, I had no idea of the responsibility, I brought this life into this world.

BARB: Have you studied and read up . . .

JOHN: I've read everything on everything.

BARB: You have? What did you read about . . . children's growing up?

JOHN: I'm an avid reader. But mainly my reading is . . . comes under those long words that don't mean a thing but that explain anthropology and archaeology, history—and I'm interested in ancient, ancient history . . . all history, but I'm particularly fond of ancient history—always was. Only after I left school (*laughter*)—not when I was at school. . . So I read everything from *Scientific American* to *East-West Journal* . . . which includes the way people behaved in tribes and how they brought up children and how they.

communicated and what the male-female roles were and all the rest of it, which I found I read anyway before there was Sean. But once I had Sean then I started looking into it from that point of view.

BARB: It sounds like you already had some philosophy about child raising before you had a child?

JOHN: No . . . whatever my so-called philosophy is about people, and children are people, and including them is the hardest thing. Considering them as people, and not as something either an extension of oneself, or as something separate from oneself THAT ONE HAS TO DEAL WITH. It's the whole concept that children and God are other than us, and I don't accept that, so based on that, I understand children, but I'm not a great parent. I try, and . . . I don't know . . . nobody knows anything about children, it seems to me. There are no experts and there're no books that really say it all. It's trial and error, as you might have heard a million times. Or you might know . . . I don't know if you've got any . . . and so therefore there's no way of finding out. But the only . . . only thing I go on is that it's another living animal that is equal to me or anybody else . . . if there's that much that one can give to another human being. . . . Am I making myself clear????

BARB: You are.

JOHN: So the concept always is basically from the Bible, and all of that Judeo-Christian story that we've been living by for two thousand years, is that God and everything is some other thing outside of ourselves—that continual us and them relationship with God, with children, with animals, with nature, the environment, where we've conquered nature, worshiped God, we deal with children, it's this separation business that I don't believe exists. It's just an idea and so I cannot separate Sean from the environment or from me or from the other end of the universe, whatever that may or may not be. That it is one living organism. So therefore however I deal with you, I deal with Sean, and vice versa. But he's not separate from me. I don't deal with my left leg any different from my right ear. I deal with the reality of the shape, and where it's placed, and how I look after, or wash different parts of the body, but I don't consider them separate.

BARB: Do you think you have any shortcomings?

JOHN: Yes, I have shortcomings as a human being. But I don't have any perfect image that I should live up to. Whether it be Jesus Christ, or Buddha, or Muhammad . . . I am, you know, just part of the whole thing. So I don't have anything to live up to. Only the best that I can conceive of.

BARB: The transition must have been incredible from self-absorption to absorption with another self.

JOHN: Well, not as big as you think, because all my work in music or in lyrics was self-absorption—all the artistic leanings are self-absorption. If it was another age I would be called a philosopher. But because I manifest as a rock-and-roll singer, therefore that word doesn't jell. But self-absorption to me isn't self-knowledge. Then if I want to express the self-knowledge, express it in a way that's best for me—which seems to be music or writing of some form or other. And when I was a child it was poetry or painting, but it's still the same thing. If you're a painter, you observe the tree and then you paint it. But it's that kind of self-knowledge, Van Gogh had self-knowledge, it may have upset him, but that's what it was . . . self-knowledge. So that's the only difference, I'm sort of always self-absorbed. But then, okay, that is included in my self-absorption then.

BARB: But it wasn't a difficult . . . an evolving process?

JOHN: Difficult inasmuch as . . . to come out of my own dream and . . . allow it . . . him to be part of it or for me to be in his dream too. That was the difficulty the same way it was with Yoko, so it was another learning process. The first learning process was to allow that she existed other than just the way I saw her . . . or thought I saw her as a female of that race and the same with the child. It's just the fact that I never thought about thinking about it before, that was the shock. "Oh, I see. Yes. Equal space. Equal time." Well, the same applies to the child so there's no such thing as too much.

BARB: Do you think there was a difference between Yoko as an equal and the way you had seen her before as maybe separate and equal? Did you see her as separate but equal?

JOHN: I just saw her like most guys had seen women all the time. Just as the female part that went along with me. The extension of me. Just whatever words we can use to describe the usual situation... that is still the usual situation... a lot has changed since. A guy with his woman.

BARB: What happens now that Sean is five? What did that mean? Does that mean that you don't have to spend as much time with him?

JOHN: Well, five means... the law says you have to exit there, right So, that's a big difference. Now, he'll have to go to school or we'll have to get a tutor, right? Five means he's survived. The first five years... are the times when you think they're gonna die all the time. The first fever. "God, he's dying. Call the doctor," or whatever and all that. Going through all that. Will he live? that was the thing. Is he going to survive, it's very dangerous... things always... it's just a physically dangerous situation at that age. And now I feel as though he can survive, you know. He's not an independent thing yet, but I can afford to say, "Well, now, daddy does something else as well." He's not quite accustomed to it yet, no. I show him where I work. And I let him come to where I work. He can see that but he'll be part of that too if he wants.

BARB: Is music as much a part of his life as you would like it to be?

JOHN: Oh, yes. I have no ambition for him other than to be healthy and know that I love him. And that Yoko and I will always be there for him. Whatever. I don't have ambition for him to be a musician or artist or anything.

BARB: But you discovered he was musical at an early age?

JOHN: Sure. The first thing I noticed in the hospital was that when the black nurses came to feed him they would put the radio on, they're not supposed to, but they do. The radio would be on all the time ... usually off the station blaring into these intensive care kids who are dying like little shriveled rabbits. Anyway, black nurses had on station WBLS, and when she fed the baby, she would hold him and give the bottle ... like the whites would come in, switch it to the country-and-western, sit down, sit there like this, smoking. So the first thing I did was ... got to get the rhythm. Whenever I fed him, I put the music on Bumm, bumm dee dummm. Now he moves like this! So in that way he was trained in music and he has my jukebox in his playroom.

BARB: A jukebox of singles?

JOHN: Yeah, full of singles like "Hound Dog," which he's into at the moment 'cause he thinks it's about rabbits and guns. You know, "Never caught a rabbit?" That's his big trip right now: hound dogs! I got the records from the fifties till right now. Maybe there's a Donna Summer or something like that. Whoever I like when I heard it on the radio. So in that way he's exposed to it all the time but he didn't see me playing a lot. He knew I played the guitar, he has a guitar but I hardly ever picked it up for the five years. It was the neighbors that turned him on to the fact that I was sort of well-known in movies. They showed him *Yellow Submarine* one Christmas at the Warner Le-Roys' next door. He came running into me: Daddy! You were singing! Were you a Beatle?" And it was, "Yes, well yes. All right."

BARB: Does he understand what Beatles were?

JOHN: He's got an idea that it was a band one time and I was in it. But it's confusing ... he doesn't know if mommy was in it. You know, did mommy and daddy do it together, because he's seen interviews of us singing together. And he's seen her singing and playing instruments together. There's no real concept of Yoko and I being separate from that. It's something happened but children have a hard time separating anything from themselves cause they're in that state before philosophy. You know, when they close their eyes, the world doesn't exist. When you go in the other room it's hard for them to conceive that you haven't vanished. It still lingers up to five.

BARB: This gets back to the original question. Is now the right time to make a record?

JOHN: Well, I felt like making a record. And Yoko wanted to do something together again.

BARB: Another question. Why a collaborative effort and not a solo?

JOHN: Because it's bloody boring.

BARB: A solo record.

JOHN Boring to do. It's boring. It is absolutely boring to be just painting in the other room. I'd sooner paint with somebody than paint by m'self. I don't need the gratification. When I first got away from the Beatles, the feeling was: to be able to have the whole album to myself, that's the answer. But then it became a chore. It became boring and you start padding it out . . . with instrumentals and stupid ditties that are . . . that have to fill up the space . . . And now, we wanted to do something together. And what could we both do best together? What do we most have in common? Music? Film? We had made a lot of movies together. But she was already into making movies so it was . . . an extension of music. And so . . . we wanted to do something together. For whatever reasons. For the five years she had to take care of business. I was taking care of the baby. And the household.

BARB: When you say "had to," she had to for the same reason that you had to? I mean certainly, Yoko didn't have to assume the responsibility . . .

JOHN: Somebody had to and I couldn't.

BARB: Why couldn't you?

JOHN: Because, I'm not capable. I'm more capable of making bread and looking after Sean and she's more capable of taking care of bankers and lawyers and deals. The Beatles thing is still an ongoing situation. It involves a lot of money and a lot of meetings and lawyers and things like that. We stopped making records together did not end the relationship.

BARB: What kind of settlement did you reach?

JOHN: A settlement is a settlement about the way certain things will be handled. It's an ongoing business. You know? It's not so much a problem...it's an ongoing business. It still produces income and somebody has to take care of it. An instead of having a lawyer for half a million or 20 million a year, or a so-called manager...she does it. So we as a unit, we consider ourselves a unit, a family unit, are taking care of our own business. Instead of asking daddy to do it in the form of some outside agency. But I don't have the capability of actually dealing with business. So her talents includes being able to do mathematics and play poker. So my talents...here she comes...my talents lie in the home. I was always a homebody. Maybe it's because I was an only child. I spent a lot of time reading. Hangin' around the home never bothered me. I enjoy it. I love it.

BARB: But at times I think you did describe yourself as an isolate. But the feeling was that you had pulled your antenna in.

JOHN: Yes. Because the messages were confused coming in as they were going out. You see the difference when I put the album out. I've withdrawn many times. Once to the Himalayas with Maharishi and all the press wrote about was look at those idiots going to Maharishi but I was sitting still as they call it in the *I-Ching* for three months in the Him...Once when we got back from Hamburg when we got deported and George had gotten deported, I didn't contact the other four for a month....that's a long time at eighteen or nineteen. Because I withdrew to think whether this is worth going on with. Now when George and Paul found out, they were mad at me. Because they thought we could have been working now. But I just withdrew. So part of me is a monk. And part is me is a performing flea. Knowing when to stop is survival for me. It's like breathing in and out for me. It happened in many forms . . . Maharishi, Janov. The sneering and the sniggering about Maharishi from the public and the press was incredible but now they're all doing it . . .

BARB: Well, it works for Janov, too.

JOHN: And for Janov, too. Somebody had a place in which I could withdraw. But now I'm old enough not to need to go somewhere with somebody to withdraw. Okay? So now I withdraw on my own.

BARB: With somebody.

JOHN: We both withdrew, yeah. But it seemed more that I'd withdrawn because she was still out, going inasmuch as meeting lawyers and people and dealing with the outside world. Where I was just being in retreat . . . with household stuff. Which is fully occupying, I'll say to all housewives, I now understand what they're screaming about. Because when I try to describe it. What I'm describing is most women's lives. I'm describing my mother's, my aunt's. Your mother's, everybody's. That's what I've been doing for five years. It just so happens that this thing called John Lennon was doing it, who used to do that . . . who was supposed to be doing something else. But what I'm telling you is that I was being just like a million, a hundred million people who are mainly female, I just went from meal to meal. Is he well? Has he brushed his teeth? Has he eaten enough vegetables? Is he overeating? Am I limiting his diet too much? Did he get some goodies? What condition is the child in? How is she when she comes back from the office? Is she going to talk to me or is she just going to talk about business?

BARB: Did that happen, too?

JOHN: Yeah, I would say, "I don't care what happened at the office today." And then I'd get the feeling that what I was doing was not important. But I say that what I was doing was damn important. I'm runnin' the machine here. This is where you're comin' back into. I'm playing that role, like the breadwinner. It was like one of those reversal comedies. I'd joke (*mincing*): "Well, how was it at the office today, dear? Do you want a little cocktail? I didn't get your slippers and your shirts are not back from the laundry yet." We see the funny side of it. That's why I can't describe what I was doing. I was doing what hundreds of millions of people are doing. I'm a rich housewife, but it still involves caring, and making sure the sheets are being looked after by whomever I employ, and that the staff all come to me with their problems. They don't go bothering Yoko, because she's dealing with the money.

BARB: So why did you stop?

JOHN: Because *this* housewife would like to have a little career for a bit. She's gonna take a job. And the air is cleared, and I'm cleared.

BARB: It just seems that life is so lubricated for you.

JOHN: Well, that's when it's time to change. It's running so smoothly we have to change the game now. To be creative . . . is to receive a gift. And I'm a craftsman who can fake it . . . like a lot of artists do. And I can reap from what I've sowed already for the rest of my life by just being a craftsman, by keeping my mouth shut and being a good boy. And I might get honored by every show-biz group and be in the Guinness book of records and get knighted. It wouldn't interest me to get it for being other than . . . for something *real* I created. For the creative spirit, the way I like it, where it's given to me, not where it's something I've made, cannot come through if the air is cluttered. The mind is cluttered. You can fake it and be a craftsman and put out paintings if you're Picasso, or records if you're a pop singer. And you might get away with it. And the business will let you get away with it. And the public will let you get away with it. You know, inside. So in order to get that clear channel open again I had to stop picking up every radio station in the world, in the universe. So my turning away from it is how I began to heal it again. I couldn't see the wood for the trees. Or I couldn't hear the music for the noise in my own head. . . . You know, Einstein or Newton, anything that was discovered was discovered by accident, by creative spirit or they were tuned into whatever came down at that moment, right? What did Einstein do, he spilled the theory of relativity when he was working on something else. He spent the rest of his life trying to prove something else, which you can never do. So what he did was really live off that record for the rest of his life. Not taking away from his brilliance or his natural native ability, but the real creation came when he sat there and something came to him or when the apple fell on his head. Newton would never have had the apple fall on his head and conceive of what it meant had he not been sitting under the tree. Daydreamin'. So for me, it's the same with music. The real music comes to me, the music of the spheres, the music that surpasses understanding, that has not to do with me, that I'm just a channel . . . So for that to come through, which is the only joy for me out of the music is for it to be given to me and I transcribe it like a medium. But I have nothing to do with it other than I'm sitting under this tree and this whole damn thing comes down and I've just put it down. That is the only joy for me. Getting into the involvement, the pretending I'm this genius who creates things or owns the rights to them, that's when it's garbage. When I'm in that illusion of thinking that somebody owes me something because I was gifted—occasionally gifted, not permanantly gifted, nobody is, occasionally gifted with this music or the words and pretending that they own it and that they should get a gold record for doing it (not that I don't appreciate adulation and awards and everything else)—but to believe it is another matter. To believe that's why I'm doing it, or just to be paid money for doing it, because as we've proved in the last five years, there's many other ways of making money. I don't have any doubt of our ability to always make money. So it's nothing to do with money. But for the joy of having the apple fall on my head every ten years or so . . . that's what I'm living for besides trying to keep the little family going, happy and progressing together. And the rest can be fun or not fun. Like this is okay. We're having fun. We're having coffee. We're talking. We're bring up stuff that I remember . . . You're enjoying it, I'm enjoying it. And we call it work. But believing in it that I own it, I created it. My record label. And my company. And my picture. Someone's stealing *MY* song . . . or they're singing my song . . . garbage. When I start believing that, that's when I'm in trouble. And that's when the gift just goes to somebody else. And one becomes a craftsman. I have nothing against craftsmen but I have no interest in being a craftsman.

BARB: Why the decision to make a commercial album?

JOHN: Because I *love* commercial music! ! I like commercials on the TV. I don't sit and watch them but as a form, if I had to do anything on TV, it would be in the style of the commercial. I like pop records. I like Olivia Newton-John singing "Magic," and Donna Summer singing whatever the hell it is she'll be singing. I like the ELO singing "All Over the World." I can dissect it and criticize it with any critic in the business. And put it down or praise it or see it from a sociological point of view or anthropological point of view . . . or any fuckin' point of view, whatever. But without any thought, I *enjoy* it. I just enjoy it! That's the kind of music I like to hear. It's folk music. I always said it and it's true. It's folk music. That's what I'm doing, folk music. I'm not intellectualizing it. I'm not arranging it into a symphony and making it into a phony art form and calling it a pop opera. Right? I'm just doing the music I enjoy. And now I'm enjoying it and it comes in the form of pop music to me. If it came in the form of painting, I'd be painting.

BARB: I know that you expect that people are going to compare this record with not only with other collaboratives but with your last record. Do you?

JOHN: *Walls and Bridges* was the last record I made. I've already compared with it. It's light-years away. Because *Walls and Bridges* . . . it's the same as cooking . . . anybody can cook rice but few can cook it well. And cooking is a manifestation of your state of mind. So is the music. There's craftsmanship in *Walls and Bridges*. There's some good. And there's the semi-sick craftsman who put together the thing. But there's no inspiration and there's misery. It's miserable. It gives off an aura of misery. Because I was miserable. So now I'm not miserable so this new album will give off an aura of not being miserable.

BARB: What about *Imagine?*

JOHN: I wasn't miserable then! Then I was with the Plastic Ono Band, which was the purest because I had been a recluse for nine or ten months, in so-called therapy . . . but I was writin' music. And clearing the channels so the damn stuff would come through.

BARB: It seemed at the time of the Plastic Ono Band that her influence was not only meditative but minimalist. The stripping away. Was that all the therapy or was it the therapy and Yoko? Is that the stripping away that you've been doing for the last five years?

JOHN: Yeah, because one accumulates a lot of garbage and it becomes apparent in your life. Even in the bedroom. If your environment is a mess, it's a manifestation of you. Society is a manifestation of all out neuroses . . . and all our messes. And on a personal level, your household and your family life and your cooking and your expression, whether it be your an executive or an artist, is a manifestation of your state of mind. So when I'm in a clear state of mind due to Yoko or therapy or a combination of them both, then it manifests itself in the music. But it's the same game of stripping down to essentials. The essentials of music to me are communication and simplicity.

BARB: What is the idea of *Double Fantasy?*

JOHN: I was walking in the Botanical Gardens in Bermuda, taking Sean and the Nanny and the household, my little kitchen entourage. We all went to lunch and I looked down and there was this flower that said, "Double fantasy." And I knew we were working on the album then anyway . . . I'm always seeing things in terms of titles. Headlines in newspapers, it's a great art. So that's what interests me. Writing was the only thing I knew, besides painting. So I enjoy communication on that kind of level. You read the headline and it cuts through the bullshit. You don't have to have a big elaborate article written by someone.

BARB: When I said your life was very lubricated you said, "What makes you think there's not stress on this album?" Is there stress? Is there a cutting edge?

JOHN: Of course there is!

BARB: What did you think of Paul's last album?

JOHN: I thought it was empty. And reflected sadness and disturbance and I think that's all I got from it. Sadness. I can't get involved in other people's music. I'm only interested in what I'm doing. But you can't live without without disturbance. There's no life without it, no matter what the old man puts out about any star, president, or presidential candidate. Everybody knows it's just a lie but we like the lie. It makes us all feel comfortable, but nobody can live without disturbance.

BARB: Where's the friction in your life?

JOHN: The friction is living. Don't be so journalistic. It's in our life, my dear. You're included. The friction is in living. In waking up every day. And getting through another day. That's where the friction is. And to express it in art is the job of the artist. And that's what I do. To express it on behalf of people who can't express it or haven't the time or ability or whatever it is. That's my job. My function in society. There's a reason for everything living. The gods that work in mysterious ways, their wonders to perform. And there's a job for flies, I'm not sure but there's a reason for it. And there's a reason for artists and musicians and it's to just do what we do. To better or lesser degrees, depending on whose opinion you follow. It's no more important or less important than anything else going on. See? But it's for the people who receive it later on. But it's for me basically and then the so called audience second. And it's just why I'm here. Just my game.

BARB: We were wondering about that the last couple of years.

JOHN: Well everybody else thinks in such short time spans. The same as when the record company used to think each Beatle record was the last one. Only the Beatles knew it wasn't. And only the Beatles knew that they would be as big as they were. The record company never caught on. They still treated them as if "We better fuck them over now in case they don't produce anything else." But I don't think like that. I knew that if I was to do it, I would do it in my own good time. Life is long. It doesn't last in terms of three months on the charts or just having a movie out or not having a movie out. So that insecurity wasn't my problem. The problem was only with wanting to have the ability to express it in my terms, the way I wanted to. So that's all. Five years. It could have been twenty years. Some guys write only one book every twenty years, other guys produce fifteen a month . . . and I don't think one's better than the other. I'm just a different kind of guy. I don't produce them every week.

BARB: In the context of how you were producing, you were producing one every year. From '69 to '74.

JOHN: They were not as clear. They got more clouded. I always thought that *Imagine* was Plastic Ono with chocolate on it, for public consumption. I'm not perfect. I have my ideals of expression or art. But life is long. I've got another forty or fifty years to be doing it. Age is irrelevant to self-expression. I don't buy that pop-star bit or movie star bit about age.

BARB: I remember Pete Hamill doing an interview with you where he said the Beatles were the custodians of childhood. I think they were for all of us. Who were yours? There was always a sense in your music a fear of growing up.

JOHN: No. I never had any fear of growing up, because. Growing up meant a fear of being . . . being told how to sit in a room. And then after being told how to sit in a room for ten or fifteen years then you're told how to go into the factory or the bank and sit in another room and always be doing what you're told. That's what the Beatles represented. To say that there is an alternative to that. That one doesn't have to and that's what artists and musicians have through life. That is their job: the longshoreman has one job, the musician another. The painter has another. It's a functional, tribal thing. We did it for a big tribe, because the communication is worldwide now. But all we did is what musicians have been doing ever since the word go. Ritualized dancing, a celebration of the seasons. The Beatles were not other than society. They were part of it. The beatles didn't lead, they were part of it.

A BEATLES REUNION?

BARB: I was surprised to hear you speak so strongly against the idea of reunion because I remember at one time you saying something to the effect that you wondered if the split was a good idea.

JOHN: I never said that ... where did you get that?

BARB: I'll give you the quote. . . .

JOHN: You give me the quote—and I'll—give the denial!

BARB: "Splitting up was a mistake in many ways" . . .

JOHN: The way we split up was the mistake— not the splitting up. .

BARB: That's a big difference. . . .

JOHN: That's a *big* difference!

BARB: That never came across in the interview.

JOHN: Well, what interview was it, because I never wanted to talk about it, you know. None of us did, really, so we would just say something glib or something just to shut people up. We couldn't say "Never," because then it would be like Ringo said once, "You're a bad guy if you're the one that says never," and God knows what would have happened anyway, right? Nobody knows what's never, it's a long time . . . . but then it goes "RINGO SAYS NEVER," big headlines, or "JOHN SAYS NEVER" or "PAUL SAYS NEVER," so nobody wanted to be the one to say "Never" and nobody wanted to be the one to say "Maybe" because then every time you said "Maybe" somebody took an ad out in the paper saying "I'm the one who's bringing them back together." So there was nothing to be said about the Beatles—it came to a point where you couldn't say a damn thing—whatever you said was something wrong—it's like being in a divorce situation, you know, you can't say anything about your ex-wife because you're in court and anything you say can be held one way or another against you or for you—so that was the situation. And the point about the Bangla Desh concert or any of these events is that if the Beatles wanted to get together, *they* would be the first to know, not the last to know. And they would be the ones that ran it, promoted it, and owned it, and it would not come from some third party outside of the four guys themselves.

BARB: Do you ever sit back with total objectivity about your music, and say that in some ways we needed the chemical component of that kind of collaboration?

JOHN: No! Because that was then, and this is now. It's like saying you needed whatever else you needed to be who or what you were, at the time you did it. What does it mean, "Did you need the chemical components to be you?"—to get through college, or to get a job at *Newsweek?* A lot of factors contributed to you getting the job at *Newsweek.* So whatever it was that made the Beatles the Beatles also made the Sixties the Sixties. The Beatles were whatever the Beatles were. And I certainly don't need it to do what I'm doing now. It could never be. Anybody that thinks that if John and Paul got together with George and Ringo, the Beatles would exist, is out of their skull!

BARB: The only reason for George and Paul to get together at all would be that in the past ten years so much is happening in your own music that it would be interesting to see what happened in the studio . . .

JOHN: It would be just as interesting if I went in the studio with Mick Jagger or Yoko Ono—I've chosen to go with Yoko Ono. *That* would be interesting. I'm not against collaborating with other people. I'm not looking to play all the instruments, you know, but I'm not looking to go back to school, and going back to the Beatles is like going back to school.

BARB: People are yearning for the good old days.

JOHN: It's garbage you know—let's dig up Glenn Miller—I mean, what the hell? He's on record! Glenn Miller exists on record! The Beatles gave everything they've got to give and more, and it exists, on record, there's no need for the Beatles—for what people think of the Beatles—the four guys that used to be that group can never, ever be that group again even if they wanted to be. You mean if Paul McCartney and John Lennon got together, would they produce some good songs? Maybe, maybe not. But whether George and Ringo joined in again is irrelevant.

BARB: Why is it irrelevant?

JOHN: *Because Paul and I created the music, okay?* So it's irrelevant. Whether it's relevant whether McCartney, Lennon and McCartney, like Rodgers and Hammerstein—instead of Rodgers and Hart or instead of Rodgers and Dingbat or whoever else they worked with—should be limited to having worked together once, to always have to be referred back to that is somebody else's problem, not mine—I never think about it. What if Paul and I got together? What the hell would it . . . it would be *boring.*

BARB: Have you been in touch with Paul?

JOHN: No, not in touch with anybody.

BARB: In a recent interview McCartney said that he thought you and Yoko had done everything you'd always wanted to do—except one . . . be yourselves.

JOHN: Paul didn't know what the fuck I was doing and he had to come up with something. He was as curious as everybody else. WHAT ARE THEY DOING THERE? WHAT DO THEY DO ALL THE TIME? I really don't know anything about how he lives, except what I read in the papers. It's been ten years since I *really* communicated with him. Shearing sheep and making lots of money—that's what the handouts say. I don't believe handouts about any artist.

BARB: Now wait a minute. I thought that Yoko said that you have seen Paul.

JOHN: Well, that was like two years—I don't

know what—three years ago? He used to turn up at the door with a guitar. So I said, do you mind ringing first, you know. I've just had a hard day with the baby. I'm worn out and you're walking in with a damn guitar.

BARB: Is there animosity?

JOHN: Why should there be? I don't have any animosity for him. I don't even think about him unless somebody brings him up. Or if some song comes out or something happens, you know, they're in the newspaper. I don't know why everyone doesn't just leave him alone—I haven't really seen him in ten years. I can talk about him forever because I know all about him, but you see, there's nothing much to say.

BARB: Why did Paul turn up at your apartment door?

JOHN: He was probably bored. Paul got what he wanted, which was total control. Maybe then he got bored with total control, because total control is isolation . . .

BARB: I guess he didn't get bored with total control, if he made the second solo album with him playing all the songs. . . .

JOHN: Well, we don't know what reason he did that for, do we? There may be multiple reasons why he did that, maybe he'd had enough of Wings by then, or whatever—I've no idea—I've no more idea than you. I don't have a problem about the Beatles, I don't have a problem about Paul, George, and Ringo, it's fine but it was then. And there are old school friends, I went to college with them, but I was never one for reunions, you know, I never went back to my old grammar school or my old art school. I'm one of those people, you know, I don't see, I don't grieve, it's all over.

BARB: What did you mean, "the way of splitting up" was a mistake?

JOHN: Because I always regretted that it had a bad taste to it.

BARB: Well, you gave it some of the bad taste.

JOHN: So? I think it could have been neater than

that. And cooler. But it just wasn't, and that's the way it was. There's many tracks, Beatles tracks, that I would redo, okay—I'd always make them all over again, they were never the way I wanted them to be, but they exist as they are, and that's what they are. So in that way, an artist is never satisfied with his work, that's the only reason to carry on doing it again.

BARB: Sounds like you're totally free and clear in your thinking of the Beatles now.

JOHN: Yeah. Well if I couldn't get free, who else the hell could? As we used to say, we were the center of the storm, we were the eye—we were calm in the middle—everyone else was crazy, not us. We were right in the center. Just sitting in rooms, like this, just talking about it, thinking up the next game. So it was everything around us that was bizarre, we weren't bizarre. Only the fact that we were the ones it was happening around was bizarre. The whole thing was bizarre, but we weren't particularly bizarre. So, it's not surprising that I can get out of it.

BARB: Even though Cynthia writes a book, and George . . .

JOHN: They all get one shot. Each chauffeur and ex-wife and ex-lover and ex-servant gets one book if they're lucky.

BARB: What about the nature of dependency and fear of loss—some of those songs are very moving songs—the one that was written in Bermuda . . .

JOHN: Most of them—99 percent of the songs written in Bermuda—all at once. Like diarrhea!

BARB: There's one song, "I'm Losing You," that sounds like it was written when you couldn't get hold of Yoko on the telephone . . .

JOHN: Right, right, exactly.

BARB: There's no communication—I remember that, "No communication" becomes a metaphor . . .

JOHN: Yes, when we were talking about the baby before, when the baby thinks you go out of the room, you vanish. . . . the moment that overwhelmed me, that I couldn't get through to her on the phone, it was overwhelming—I just felt completely out there, so I did what I always do, which is either paint it, draw it or sing it.

BARB: Sounds like the fantasy IS the loss . . .

JOHN: Yes, the fantasy is the loss; you can say, "Oh well, is it?" I never know what I'm talking about until a year later when I see what I'm writing. Some of it, even the Beatles stuff, when I hear it now, I think, Oh, that's what . . . and I think Dylan once said it about his work—he was really talking about himself— a lot of it in the early days, it was "him" and "you" and "they" that were doing things, but really when I look back on it, it's *me* I'm talking about. And so, yes, you could say it was overwhelming, that I actually felt out in the universe you know, disconnected, and so I converted it into that. But it also could be a short story about when we were physically separated in the early seventies, you can apply it to that too—although I wasn't thinking that at the time. It described that situation, too, of being kicked out of the nest and being dead. Or being not connected is like being dead. There's that difference—being alone and being lonely is two different things. Something I've learned in the past ten years. What I did in the past ten years was rediscover that I was John Lennon before the Beatles, and after the Beatles, and so be it.

BARB: Do you have such a strong memory of being John Lennon before the Beatles?

JOHN: Yes. That's what I did in the past five years. One moment—the actual moment when I remembered who I was—completely, not in glimpses—I never really lost complete touch with myself—but a lot of the time I did, for long periods of time. . . . I was in a room in Hong Kong, because Yoko had sent me on a trip round the world by myself, and I hadn't done anything by myself since I was twenty. I didn't know how to call for room service, check into a hotel—this sounds—if somebody reads this and they think, Well these fucking artists, or These bloody pop stars, or These actors, you know, and they don't understand . . . the *pain* of being a freak. . . .

BARB: What do you mean, Yoko sent you?

JOHN: She said "Why don't you do this?" I said "Really? By myself? Hong Kong? Singapore?" I said "But what if . . ."

BARB: Doesn't sound like much fun . . . sounds like anticipation of some anxiety attack. . . .

JOHN: Well, yeah, I'm like that you know— "What if people bother me?"—and well I had a big excuse for it you see, I had to isolate using Being Famous as an immense excuse. An incredible excuse. For never facing anything. Because I was Famous— therefore I can't go to the movies, I can't go to the theater, I can't do anything. So sitting in this room, taking baths, which I'd noticed Yoko do, and women do, every time I got nervous, I took a bath. It's a great female trick, it's a great one. I must have had about forty baths . . . and I'm looking out over the Hong Kong bay, and there's something that's like ringing a bell, it's like what is it? What is it? And then I just got very very relaxed. And it was like a recognition. God! It's me! This relaxed person is *me.* I remember this guy from way back when! This feeling is from way, way, way back when. I know what the fuck I'm doing! I know who I am—it doesn't rely on any outside agency or adulation, or nonadulation, or achievement or nonachievement, or hit record or no hit record. Or anything. It's absolutely irrelevant whether the teacher loves me, hates me—I'm still me. *He* knows how to do things—*he* knows how to get around—*he* knows how to form a group—*he* knows how to do everything he wants to do—WOW! So I called, I said "Guess who, it's ME! It's ME here. "I walked out of that hotel, I just followed the workers onto the ferry, nobody noticed me . . . this is an aside thing: somebody asked a very famous actress, and I've forgotten who it was, somebody like Carole Lombard, somebody really big from way back, and maybe this story came over Johnny Carson—but they asked her how one actress couldn't get down the street without being recognized and the other one could, when they were both equally famous. And she said, "This is how I do it," and she demonstrated. She walked down the street as Carole Lombard, and everybody turned their heads—and then she walked down the street as nobody. And that works. I CAN get around. If I'm supernervous, I send out a vibe, "Here's a nervous person coming!" so they're going to look round because of this vibration that's walking past, and then afterward say "It's somebody famous." Because some people are like that anyway. So I got out, and I got on the ferry. Looking around. It's like a thrill, I'm walking around all by myself, and I'm in the middle of the Far East, and all these people are going to work, you know there's Europeans and Chinese and everybody and they're all just going to work and we get along over to Kao Lung, and I just followed the crowd because I didn't know where the hell I was, having never seen anything—I've just been in a hotel in Hong Kong, and I just wandered around, and when I saw them dispersing into offices or different things, I just went into the little cafes and ate, [gestures] this and that, "Give me two" and all that bit, then I went to the stores and I bought things—I did that for a few days because I didn't try and adjust to their time, I was always up at five o'clock, watch the sun come up and walk out and wander round Hong Kong at dawn. And it was just fantastic.

BARB: Did you enjoy the aloneness?

JOHN: I loved it! I loved it—that's what I rediscovered, the feeling that I used to have as a youngster, I remember another incident in my life when I was walking in the mountains of Scotland, up in the north, I was with an auntie, who had a house up there, and I remember this feeling coming over me, you know, I thought, This is what they call poetic, or whatever they call it. When I looked back I realized I was kind of hallucinating. You know, when you're walking along and the ground starts going beneath you and the heather, and I could see this mountain in the distance, and this kind of FEELING came over me—I thought, This is SOMETHING. What is this? Ah, this is that one they're always talking about, the one that makes you paint or write, because it's so overwhelming that you want to tell somebody, and you can't describe it, you can't say "There's this feeling that I'm having and the world looks like . . . and it's sort of glowing . . . and there's a . . ." so you have to try and paint it, right, or put it into poetry or something like that. Well it was that same kind of thing. But it was recognition that the thing had been with me all my life. And that's why maybe I got a little like that when you said about Putting the Boys Back Together Again—it's irrelevant you know! Because the feeling was with me before the Beatles and with me after. And it's absolutely—the feeling is something that you either recognize . . .

BARB: And have . . .

JOHN: Well, everybody has it, but most people just won't allow it to come in. Daydreaming is forbidden in school. That's what I was talking about—schools—earlier, I daydreamed my way through the whole school. I just absolutely was in a trance for twenty years because it was absolutely boring. If I wasn't in a trace, I wasn't there—I was at the movies, or running around.

BARB: That sounds like something from "Watching the Wheels."

JOHN: Right, because that's what I'm saying—what "Watching the Wheels" is saying—all these teachers, which you can call critics, media, friends-in-the business, other singers—that have been commenting about me for eight years, they've all had something to say about me, I'm thrilled that they're all so concerned, but there isn't one of them that hasn't made some remark about one way or the other—so they're all talking. Now to me, it just sounds like the teachers—if I look through my report card, it's the same thing. "Too content to get a cheap laugh hiding behind this," or "Daydreaming his life away." Am I getting this from those rock and rollers and these rock-and-roll critics? And the do-gooders and the rest of them? Well, it's ringing a bell in my head, I'm sitting there picking this up, because I ain't doing nothing, I'm watching the wheels, everyone's talking about me, I ain't doing nothing. "Lennon sit up," "Lennon sit down," "Lennon do your homework," "Lennon you're a bad boy," "Lennon you're a good boy," what the hell is this? I heard this before somewhere . . . I heard it at school! So this period was that—to reestablish me as me, for myself. That's why I'm free of the Beatles. Because I took time to free myself. Mentally from it, and look at what it is. And now I know. So here I am, right? That's it! It's beautiful, you know, it's just like walking those hills.

"Some people are saying that this is the end of an era, but what we said before still stands—the eighties will be a beautiful decade. John loved and prayed for the human race. Please tell people to pray the same for him. Please remember that he had deep faith and love for life and that, though he has now joined the greater force, he is still with us."

—Yoko Ono
December 1980

8

CHRONOLOGY: LIVERPOOL TO NEW YORK, 1940-80

1940

July 7: Richard Starkey (Ringo Starr) was born at 9 Madryn Street, Dingle, Liverpool, England.

October 9: John Winston Lennon was born in Oxford Street Maternity Hospital, Liverpool, England.

1942

June 18: James Paul McCartney was born at Walton Hospital, England.

1943

February 25: George Harrison was born at 12 Arnold Grove, Wavetree, Liverpool, England.

1955

Early: In his fifth form at the Quarrybank Grammar School in Liverpool, John Lennon formed a musical group, the Quarrymen.

June 15: John Lennon and Paul McCartney were introduced by a mutual friend at a church social in Woolton, Liverpool. Paul played with the Quarrymen on stage, at the affair.

1956

October 31: Mrs. Mary McCartney, Paul's mother, died of cancer at the age of forty-seven.

1958

July 15: John Lennon's mother was killed in a Liverpool car accident.

August 29: George Harrison joined the Quarrymen on the opening night of the Casbah Club in Liverpool. The club was in the basement of Pete Best's house, and he sat in on the drums with the group.

The Remainder of the year: Later in the year, the Quarrymen changed their name to Johnny and the Moondogs. Throughout that time, drummers other than Pete Best, such as Johnny Hutch and Tommy Moore, also played with the group. Toward the end of the year, Lennon left home and took an apartment near the Liverpool College of Art, where he was a student.

1959

1959: Johnny and the Moondogs (John, Paul, and George) performed on the Caroll Levis *Discoveries* TV show. Soon after, the group changed its name to the Silver Beatles.

1960

Mid-1960: John and Paul separated briefly from the group and appeared for one performance as the Nurk Twins.

December 27: They played a special "welcome home" concert at the Litherland Town Hall.

1961

March 21: The Beatles made their debut at the Cavern, in Liverpool.

April: The group made their third trip to Hamburg,

where they recorded with Tony Sheridan, a British singer, for Polydor.

October: Brian Epstein, owner of the Nems record store, received a number of requests for the Beatles' record, "My Bonnie," but when he tried to order the record, he found that it was not available in England.

November 9: Epstein saw the Beatles for the first time, at the Cavern.

December: Epstein invited the group over to his shop, where imported copies of their records had been selling out. Later in the month, the Beatles signed their first contract with Epstein.

1962

January 1: The Beatles went to London to test for Decca, but they were turned down.

January: The Beatles were signed to play on the opening night of the Star Club, in Hamburg. That same month the Beatles were picked as the top group in a popularity poll sponsored by the publication *Merseybeat*.

April 5: The Cavern hosted a Beatles Fan Club Night before their fourth trip to Hamburg. Stu Sutcliffe, a bass player and friend of the group who had stayed on in Hamburg, died of a brain hemorrhage the night before they arrived in Hamburg.

June 6: The Beatles passed an audition with George Martin, of E.M.I.

June 11: The Beatles made their first BBC radio broadcast, from Manchester, where they were accompanied by fans from the Cavern.

June 26: Brian Epstein formed his company. Nems Enterprises Ltd.

August 1: The group appeared at the Cavern with Gerry and the Pacemakers, and the Merseybeats. Pete Best was asked to resign from the group and Ringo took his place. Previously, Ringo had been with another Liverpool group, Rory Storm and the Hurricanes.

August 23: John Lennon married Cynthia Powell in Liverpool, with Paul McCartney as his best man.

September: The group went to London, to E.M.I.'s studios, where they were signed by George Martin and where they recorded "Love Me Do" and "P.S. I Love You."

October 1: The Beatles signed their second contract with Brian Epstein, and they appointed him manager for a period of five years.

October 5: Their first single, recorded in September was released in Britain on the Parlophone label.

November 26: The group recorded their second single, "Please Please Me."

December 18: They began their fifth and final session at the Star Club, in Hamburg.

1963

January 11: Their second single record of "Please Please Me" and "Ask Me Why" was released in Britain on Parlophone. On that same day, they appeared on the television program *Thank Your Lucky Stars* on BBC-TV in Britain.

February 2: They began their first nationwide tour of Britain, backing up singer Helen Shapiro. Danny Williams and Kenny Lunch also appeared.

February 19: "Please Please Me" became their first number one hit single in England.

February 26: Their publishing company, Northern Songs Ltd, was formed. The company's directors were John Lennon, Paul McCartney, Brian Epstein, and Dick James. The first song published was "From Me to You."

March 7: The LP *Please Please Me* was released in the United Kingdom by Parlophone.

April 8: John Charles Julian Lennon was born at the Sefton General Hospital, and later on taken home to Liverpool, where John and his wife Cynthia were living with his Aunt Mimi.

April 12: The Beatles' third single, "From Me to You" and "Thank You Girl" was released in the U.K. on the Parlophone label.

April 26: "Do You Want to Know a Secret" and "I'll Be On My Way" were recorded by Billy J. Kramer and released on Parlophone. Both were written by John and Paul.

April: The Beatles appeared at the *New Musical Express* poll winners' concert, and soon after left for a twelve-day holiday in the Canary Islands.

May 18: The group headlined their own national tour with Roy Orbison and Gerry and the Pacemakers.

July 16: The BBC radio series *Pop Go the Beatles* was returned to the air for ten more weeks, lasting for a total of fifteen weeks.

July 26: Parlophone released the EP (extended play record) *The Beatles* (*No. 1*) in Britain; with over 100,000 advance orders waiting. On the same day, Billy J. Kramer, a singer groomed by Brian Epstein, released "Bad to Me," which was written by John and Paul. Also released by Kramer on Parlophone was "I Call Your Name."

August: The Beatles appeared at the Cavern for the last time, in a show with the Escorts and the Merseybeats.

August: The group's fourth single, "She Loves You" and "I'll Get You," was released on Parlophone, in Britain.

August 31: The Fourmost were introduced by Brian Epstein on the Parlophone label with the song "Hello Little Girl," written by John and Paul.

September 6: Brian Epstein signed his first female singer, Cilla Black, and announced that she would debut with the Lennon/McCartney song "Love of the Loved," on Parlophone. At the same time, Parlophone released an EP by the Beatles with the songs "Please Please Me," "From Me to You," "Thank You Girl," and "Love Me Do."

September 7: "She Loves You" reached the number one spot on the *Melody Maker* chart, and occupied that position for seven weeks.

End of September: John Lennon vacationed in Paris.

October: An EP released by Parlophone included the tracks "I Saw Her Standing There," "Misery," "Chains," and "Anna (Go to Him)." The group began a brief Scottish tour.

October 11: "She Loves You" became their first gold record, with sales of over 1 million. It was also announced that sales of the *Please Please Me* album had passed the quarter million mark.

October 13: Beatlemania! The Beatles appeared on *Sunday Night at the London Palladium* and their fans rioted outside.

November 4: The Beatles appeared on the Royal Variety Show at the Prince of Wales Theatre in London. The performance was attended by the Queen Mother, Princess Margaret, and Lord Snowdon, and was highlighted by Lennon's famous instructions to the audience: "Those of you in the cheaper seats—clap your hands; and those of you in the more expensive seats—just rattle your jewelry."

November 10: Film of the Royal Variety Show performance was syndicated by ITV and seen by millions.

November 22: Awaited by some 300,000 advance orders, the group's second LP, *With the Beatles,* was released in Britain by Parlophone.

November 30: Parlophone released their fifth single, "I Want to Hold Your Hand" and "This Boy," to over one-half million advance orders.

December: It was reported that the Beatles gave Capital the first option for the distribution of their records in the U.S.

December 23: Radio Luxembourg began broadcasting a weekly show called *It's the Beatles.*

End of December: John Lennon and Paul McCartney were hailed as the outstanding English composers of 1963, by the *Times* of London.

December 29: WMCA in New York City broadcast the first Beatles song in the U.S. "I Want to Hold Your Hand."

1964

January 3: The Beatles' first TV appearance in the United States. Film clips from a concert were shown on the *Jack Paar Show.*

January 13: Capitol released the first Beatles record in the U.S., the single "I Want to Hold Your Hand"/"I Saw Her Standing There."

Mid-January: "I Want to Hold Your Hand" hit number one in Australia.

January 20: Capitol released the LP *Meet the Beatles* in the United States.

End of January: "She Loves You" was released in the United States by Swan Records.

February: The single "Please Please Me"/"Ask Me Why" was released in the U.S. by the Vee Jay record company. Soon thereafter, the single "Twist and

Shout"/ "There's a Place" was also released in the U.S. by Vee Jay.

The *All My Loving* EP, including "Money," "P.S. I Love You," and "Ask Me Why," was released in the U.S. by Vee Jay.

The *All My Loving EP,* including "Money," "P.S. I Love You," and "Ask Me Why," was released in England by Parlophone.

February 7: Thousands of fans greeted the Beatles at Kennedy Airport in New York, as did swarms of the press. Riots occurred outside the Plaza Hotel, where they stayed.

February 9: The *Ed Sullivan Show* debut. The Beatles opened with "All My Loving," "Till There Was You," and "She Loves You." The group then came back for a second spot and did "I Saw Her Standing There" and "I Want to Hold Your Hand."

February 11: The group gave their first live concert in the U.S., at the Washington Coliseum, where they appeared with the Caravelles, Tommy Roe, and the Chiffons.

February 12: Back in New York, the group gave two performances at Carnegie Hall, both of which had sold out almost immediately.

February 15: The group spent the day rehearsing for their second appearance on the *Ed Sullivan Show,* which was scheduled for the next day.

February 16: From the Deauville Hotel in Miami Beach, the Beatles made their second hit appearance on the *Ed Sullivan Show.*

February 21: The Beatles were voted show business personalities of the year by the Variety Club of Great Britain.

February 22: The group returned to Great Britain.

February 28: "Cry for a Shadow," written by Harrison and Lennon, and with Pete Best on drums, was released by Polydor in the U.K. On the flipside was "Why," sung by Tony Sheridan and backed up by the Beatles. Both songs had been recorded earlier, in Hamburg, in 1961.

March 2: The Beatles began work on their first film, *A Hard Day's Night,* shot on location in Liverpool.

March 13: The Beatles held the top four slots on the *Cash Box* charts, with (1) "She Loves You," (2) "I Want to Hold Your Hand," (3) "Please Please Me," and (4) "Twist and Shout."

The LP *Meet the Beatles* had sold over 3.5 million copies in the Unites States, making it the largest-selling LP of all times. Awaiting the Beatles' next single release, "Can't Buy Me Love," were advanced orders in the U.S. in excess of 1.5 million.

March 20: Parlophone released the Beatles' sixth single, "Can't Buy Me Love"/"You Can't Do That," in England. On the day of the release, the group appeared on Rediffusion TV's *Ready, Steady, Go,* with Dusty Springfield.

March 23: John Lennon got his first book published: *John Lennon in His Own Write.*

End of March: The Beatles captured the top six spots of the Australian Top Ten with (1) "I Saw Her Standing There," (2) "Love Me Do," (3) "Roll Over Beethoven," (4) "All My Loving," (5) "She Loves You," and (6) "I Want to Hold Your Hand."

March 30: The single "Can't Buy Me Love"/"You Can't Do That" was released in the U.S. by Capitol.

April 6: The Billboard chart was led by (1) "Can't Buy Me Love," (2) "Twist and Shout," (3) "She Loves You," (4) "I Want to Hold Your Hand," and (5) "Please Please Me."

April 10: Capitol released the Beatles' second album in the U.S., called *The Beatles' Second Album.*

April 16: Ed Sullivan's interview of the group on the set of *A Hard Day's Night* was to be broadcast on his television show.

End of April: John Lennon in His Own Write was published in the U.S. by Simon and Schuster.

May 6: The American disk jockey Murry the K hosted the Rediffusion TV show *Around the Beatles*, which also featured Millie, Long John Baldry and Cilla Black.

May 11: An EP of "Roll Over Beethoven"/"All My Lovin"/"This Boy"/"Please Mr. Postman" was released by Capitol in the United States.

Mid-May: "Love Me Do" was released in the United States by Vee Jay. Although it achieved only moderate success in Britain, the song very quickly reached number one on the *Cash Box* chart in the U.S. The flip side was "P.S. I Love You."

May 29: "Ain't She Sweet," which was sung by John Lennon and backed up by the Beatles, was released by Polydor in Britain. On the flipside is "If You Love Me Baby," sung by Tony Sheridan. Subsequently, the single was released by Atco in the U.S.

May 31: Back from a month's vacation, the Beatles gave two concerts at the Prince of Wales Theatre in London.

June 3: Ringo Starr fell ill with tonsilitis. Jimmy Nicol substituted for him as the group headed off for a tour.

June 6: Tens of thousands of fans thronged the streets of Amsterdam, and the Beatles held a live concert.

June 12: The Australian tour began in Adelaide, and Jimmy Nicol remained with the group for the first two concerts. Ringo rejoined the group a few days later, in Melbourne, with thousands of fans on hand to greet him. Later on, a quarter of a million saw the group pass through the streets of Melbourne by car.

June 19: Long Tall Sally, an EP, was released by Parlophone in the U.K.

Polydor released an LP, *The Beatles' First.* Most of the album was recorded in Hamburg, in 1961, with Pete Best as drummer. (Never released in the U.S.).

June 26: The LP *A Hard Day's Night* was released in the U.S. by United Artists.

End of June: The Beatles flew to Brisbane for the final stop on their Australian tour.

July 2: The group returned to London.

July 6: The film *A Hard Day's Night* premiered at the London Pavillion.

July 8: The group appeared on *Top of the Pops,* their first BBC-TV appearance in over six months.

July 10: Tens of thousands of fans waited in the Liverpool streets to welcome the Beatles home from their tour, and to celebrate the northern premiere of *A Hard Day's Night.*

The group's seventh single, "A Hard Day's Night" and "Things We Said Today," was released in Britain by Parlophone, as was their LP *A Hard Day's Night.*

July 12: The group appeared once again on the *Ed Sullivan Show,* in film clips from *A Hard Day's Night.*

July 13: Capitol Records released the single "A Hard Day's Night"/"I Should Have Known Better" in the U.S.

July 20: Capitol Records released the Beatles' LP *Something New,* as well as two singles. "I'll Cry Instead"/"I'm Just Happy to Dance with You" and "And I Love Her"/"If I Fell," all in the United States.

July: John Lennon bought a house on St. George's Hill, in Weybridge.

July 23: In a charity show called the *Night of 100 Stars,* held at the London Palladium, the Beatles appeared with Sir Laurence Olivier, Dame Edith Evans, and Shirley Bassey.

July 29: During a concert in Stockholm, John and Paul suffered from serious electrical shocks.

July 30: They returned from Stockholm.

July 31: Parlophone released "It's for You," which was written by John and Paul and sung by Cilla Black.

August 12: A Hard Day's Night opened in the U.S.

August 14: The trade press reported that more prints of *A Hard Day's Night* had been made than for any other film in history.

August 19: The Beatles began their second tour of the U.S., planning performances in eighteen states.

August 24: Capitol Records released the single "Slow Down"/"Matchbox" in the United States.

September 11: Before they arrived in Jacksonville, Florida, the Beatles announced that they would not play to a segregated audience. Lennon is quoted as saying: "We never play to segregated audiences, and we're not going to start now. I'd rather lose our appearance money."

September 19: Lennon gave permission for his cartoon drawing, "The Fat Budgie" to be printed as a Christmas card.

September 20: Once again, the Beatles appeared on the *Ed Sullivan Show*. The group also appeared at a charity concert in New York for cerebral palsy victims.

September 25: Brian Epstein announces that he had turned down an offer of 3.5 million pounds sterling from a syndicate of American businessmen for his interest in the Beatles.

October: A Cellar Full of Noise, by Brian Epstein, was published by Souvenir Press.

October 16: The single "If I Fell" and "Tell Me Why" was released by Parlophone outside of Great Britain. On that day, the group appeared on Rediffusion TV's *Ready, Steady, Go.*

October 25: The Beatles won five major Ivor Novello awards: (1) for the most outstanding contribution to British music in 1963, (2) for the most broadcast song ("She Love You"), (3) for the top-selling record "She Loves You"), (4) for the second top-selling record ("I want to Hold Your Hand"), and (5) for the second most-outstanding song ("All My Loving").

November: The EP *A Hard Day's Night* was released by Parlophone, in the U.K.

November 23: Capital Records released the LP *The Beatles' Story* and the single "I feel Fine"/"She's a Woman" in the U.S.

November 27: Parlophone released the group's eighth single, "I Feel Fine" and "She's a Woman." On the same day they appeared on Rediffusion TV's *Ready, Steady, Go.*

December 4: An new LP, *Beatles for Sale,* was released by Parlophone in Britain.

December 15: Capitol released the LP *Beatles '65* in the U.S.

December: E.M.I. announced that *Beatles for Sale* had sold almost 750,000 copies in Britain in two weeks.

December 24: The Beatles' Christmas show opened. With them appeared Freddie and the Dreamers, Jimmy Savile, Sounds Incorporated, the Yardbirds, Ray Fell, and Elkie Brooks. All members of the fan club received special Christmas disks.

December 26: The Beatles appeared on the BBC Light Programme's *Saturday Club.*

December: Ringo's tonsils were removed.

1965

January 9: John Lennon appeared on BBC-2 and read his poems.

January 19: It is reported that out of seven golden records awarded in the U.S. in 1964, the Beatles received four: (1) "I Want to Hold Your Hand," (2) "Can't Buy Me Love," (3) "A Hard Day's Night," and (4) "I Feel Fine."

February 1: Capitol released the EP of "Honey Don't"/"I'm a Loser"/"Mr. Moonlight"/"Everybody's Trying to Be My Baby" in the United States.

February 11: Ringo Starr married Maureen Cox in London. John, his wife Cynthia, and George attended, but Paul was in the United States.

February 15: Capitol released the single "Eight Days a Week"/"I Don't Want to Spoil the Party" in the U.S.

February 12: The Beatles left for the Bahamas to film their second movie, *Help!*

March 22: The Early Beatles, a Capitol LP, was released in the U.S.

April 9: The Beatles' ninth single, "Ticket to Ride" and "Yes It Is," was released in England by Parlophone.

April 11: The Beatles appeared at the annual *New Musical Express* poll winner's concert, and then on the same day they also appeared on the *Eamonn Andrews Show, on* BBC-TV in Britain.

April 19: The single of "Ticket to Ride"/"Yes It Is" was released in the U.S. by Capitol.

May 10: "Dizzy Miss Lizzie" and "Bad Boy," two songs by Larry Williams, were recorded by the group for release on an upcoming American album.

May 12: Help! was finished.

June 4: An EP, *Beatles for Sale (No. 2)* was released by Parlophone in England.

June: It was reported that over 1300 different versions of Beatles' songs had been recorded, not including recordings in South America, India, and Africa, for which no figures were available.

June 12: The Beatles were awarded the M.B.E. (Most Excellent Order of the British Empire).

June: A dispute over the awarding of the M.B.E. to the Beatles followed. War heroes such as Paul Pearson and government officials such as Canadian M.P. Hector Dupuis sent their M.B.E.'s back, in protest. Others followed suit. Some high officials such as the British High Commissioner to Australia, Lieutenant General Sir William Oliver, defended the award being made to the Beatles.

June 14: Capitol released the LP *Beatles VI* in the U.S.

June: Lennon appeared on BBC-TV's *Tonight,* and promoted his book *A Spaniard in the Works.* More M.B.E.'s were returned.

June 21: Author Richard Pape returned his M.B.E. and criticized the Beatles for debasing the royal honors list.

June 24: *A Spaniard in the Works* was published, and on the same day an interview with Lennon was shown on *Today* on ITV.

June 24: The Beatles' first Italian appearance took place in Milan, to many empty seats. The tour proceeded on to Rome, and then the Côte d'Azur.

July 19: Capitol released the single "Help!"/"I'm Down" in the U.S.

July 23: Parlophone released the group's tenth single, "Help!" and "I'm Down" in England.

July 29: Help! premiered, with Princess Margaret and Lord Snowdon in attendance. The proceeds were donated to charity.

August 3: Subafilms, the group's film company, announced that it was going to make a movie of the National Jazz Festival in Richmond, Virginia. The Who, the Yardbirds, the Moody Blues, Georgie Fame, Manfred Mann, Rod Stewart, and Spencer Davis starred. The film was eventually shown on television in the United States.

August 6: The *Help!* LP was released by Parlophone in Great Britain.

John bought a cottage for his Aunt Mimi near the town of Bournemouth.

August 13: The Beatles left for the U.S. On the same day, Capitol released the LP *Help!* in America.

August 15: They gave a concert at Shea Stadium, New York, for an audience of 56,000. The concert was introduced by Ed Sullivan.

August 24: Northern Songs, the group's publishing company, reported profits for the year in excess of 600,000 pounds sterling.

September 1: The Beatles returned to London.

September 12: The group appeared on the *Ed Sullivan Show*.

September 13: Capitol released the single of "Yesterday"/"Act Naturally" in the U.S.

October 1: Paul McCartney's "Yesterday" hit number one on both *Cash Box* and *Billboard* charts.

October 22: The group declined to appear in the Royal Variety Show, opting instead to donate the proceeds from one of their shows to charity.

October 26: The Beatles were invested with their M.B.E.'s by the Queen, at Buckingham Palace. Years later, John was quoted as saying that they had smoked marijuana in the palace lavatory, and had been high during their presentation to the queen.

November 13: It is reported that while in the United States, Epstein persuaded Capitol not to release the single "Boys" and "Kansas City," because he felt the music incompatible with the groups developing style.

December 1: The LP *Rubber Soul* was released by Parlophone, in England.

December 3: Their eleventh single, "Day Tripper" and "We Can Work It out," was released in the U.K. by Parlophone.

December 6: Capitol released the LP *Rubber Soul* and the single "We Can Work It Out"/"Day Tripper" in the United States.

December 31: Freddie Lennon, John's father, had two songs released by Pye: "That's My Life (My Love and My Home)" and "The Next Time You Feel Important."

1966

January 21: George Harrison married Patti Boyd in Epsom. Paul McCartney was the only other Beatle in attendance.

January 28: Epstein's agency, Nems, was reported to have merged with or acquired the Vic Lewis Organization. This made Brian Epstein the representative of Matt Munro and of Donovan, and the British agent for Johnny Mathis, the Supremes, Herb Alpert, Pat Boone, Tony Bennett, and other top American performers.

February 4: It was announced that the Beatles had been awarded three gold records in the U.S., for "Help!" "Eight Days a Week," and "Yesterday."

February 7: Capitol released the single "Nowhere Man" and "What Goes On" in the U.S.

March 1: The film of the Beatles' concert at Shea Stadium was shown on BBC.

May 1: The Beatles appeared at the annual *New Musical Express* poll winners concert. This was to be their last live appearance on stage as the Beatles in Britain.

May 23: Capitol released the single "Paperback Writer" and "Rain" in the U.S.

June 10: The Beatles' twelfth single, "Paperback Writer" and "Rain," was released by Parlophone in Great Britain.

June 16: It was reported that the record jacket for the American LP *"Yesterday" . . . and Today* had been withdrawn as too offensive. The picture had shown the Beatles dressed up like butchers, standing around the severed head of a doll. On that same day, the group made a surprise live appearance on *Top of the Pops.*

June 20: Capitol released the LP *"Yesterday" . . . and Today* in the U.S.

June 22: Backed by George Harrison and Sir William Pigott-Brown, Sibylla's discotheque opened in London. The Beatles and the Rolling Stones attended the opening.

June 24: The Beatles gave two concerts in Munich, one taped for German television. Also in the show were Cliff Bennett and the Rebel Rousers, and Peter and Gordon.

June 26: The group gave two concerts in Hamburg. The fans rioted and the police had to be called in.

June 30: In Tokyo, there were over 200,000 applications for 10,000 seats. One of the concerts was filmed for NTV, of Japan.

July 3: Fifty thousand fans greeted the Beatles in Manila.

July 4: The Beatles played to their largest audience ever, estimated at 100,000 in Manila. Unfortunately, however, later that day the group failed to appear at a party at the presidential palace, by mistake. This was taken as an insult to the president, and as the group tried to leave the airport, they were attacked and booed by the crowd.

July 8: The Beatles returned to London, swearing that they would never return to the Philippines.

July 12: Three major Ivor Novello awards went to Lennon and McCartney, for (1) top selling single of 1965, "We Can Work It Out"; (2) most outstanding song of 1965, "Yesterday"; and (3) second-best-selling single, "Help!"

July 23: British Prime Minister Harold Wilson was on hand for the reopening of the Cavern, along with the lord mayor of Liverpool and a host of other government and popular celebrities. The Beatles sent a telegram.

July 29: The Beatles turned down an offer to tour South Africa.

August: Lennon's inflammatory remarks concerning Christianity began to stir protest. In an interview with the London *Evening Standard,* he had said, "Christianity will go. It will go. It will vanish and shrink. I needn't argue about that. I'm right and I will be proved right. We are more popular than Jesus now. I don't know which will go first—rock and roll or Christianity. Jesus was all right, but his disciples were thick and ordinary." In response, the disk jockeys of Birmingham, Alabama announced their intention to make a bonfire of Beatles records, photographs, and other memorabilia.

August 4: It was reported that Beatles records had been banned by radio stations in New York, Texas, Utah, and South Carolina.

August 5: The Beatles' thirteenth single, "Yellow Submarine" and "Eleanor Rigby," was released by Parlophone in Britain and Capitol in the U.S. Also on that day, Parlophone released the LP *"Revolver"* in the U.K. Three days later (August 8). *Revolver* was released by Capitol in the U.S.

August 6: Thirty American radio stations had banned all Beatles records because of Lennon's remarks. In New York, Brian Epstein apologized for any offense given.

August 11: The Beatles arrived in the United States, and Lennon apologized. When asked, however, if he had called America a racist country, McCartney affirmed that this was true.

August 12: What was to be the Beatles' third and last American concert tour opened successfully in Chicago.

August 17: In Toronto, Lennon said that he was in favor of Americans fleeing to Canada to avoid the draft.

August 19: The Beatles' concert in Memphis was picketed by the Ku Klux Klan.

August 23: The Beatles' concert at Shea Stadium was again a sellout.

August 28: A crowd in Los Angeles rioted, and the group escaped in an armored car.

August 29: The Beatles made their final appearance together, as a group, in San Francisco, at Candlestick Park.

August 31: The group returned to London.

September 1: John Lennon donated one of his Christmas card designs to charity, to Action for the Crippled Child.

September 19: John Lennon flew to Spain, to film in a movie called *How I Won the War.*

November 11: In an interview, Ringo denied that the group had thoughts of splitting up.

November: John met Yoko Ono, at an art exhibit held by her at the Indica Gallery in London.

November 14: Brian Epstein denied reports that Allen Klein was being considered for the future management of two of the Beatles. A spokesman for Mr. Klein, however, acknowledged that it was true.

November 24: The Beatles again started to record together.

December 9: The LP *Oldies (But Goldies)* was released by Parlophone in Britain.

December 18: The Family Way, a movie starring John and Hayley Mills, premiered in London, and Paul McCartney was the solo composer of the music.

December 26: John Lennon appeared in a skit on Peter Cook and Dudley Moore's show *Not Only ... But Also.*

December 29: Billboard reported that the Beatles were on top of the charts in thirteen countries around the world, and that they were second or third in most other countries.

1967

January 7: It was reported that in 1966, the Beatles had six gold records in the U.S.

January 10: The Beatles at Shea Stadium showed on American TV.

January 21: The Nems organization merged with the Robert Stigwood organization, bringing the Who, Cream, the Merseys, and Crispian St. Peters into the fold.

January 30: The Beatles attended a concert given by the Who and Jimi Hendrix.

February 31: Capitol released the single "Strawberry fields Forever"/"Penny Lane" in the U.S.

February 17: The group's fourteenth single, "Penny Lane" and "Strawberry Fields Forever," was released by Parlophone, in the U.K. To promote the disk, the group appeared on a special film clip aired on the BBC's *Top of the Pops;* it was eventually shown worldwide.

February 25: Promotional clips for "Penny Lane"/"Strawberry Fields" aired on *Hollywood Palace* (U.S.)

March 11: Lennon and McCartney won the Grammy Award for composing "Michelle," which was voted Song of the Year. McCartney also won a Grammy for the best contemporary solo vocal performance on "Eleanor Rigby." Klaus Voorman won one for the cover of *Revolver.*

March 25: The Beatles won two more Ivor Novello awards, one for the most performed work of 1966, "Michelle," and another for top-selling single of 1966, "Yellow Submarine."

May 20: The BBC banned the song "A Day in the Life" (due out on the upcoming *Sgt. Pepper* LP) because it might encourage drug abuse. The Beatles argued that this was a misinterpretation.

May 27: Lennon announced that the band's touring days were over.

June 1: The LP *Sgt. Pepper's Lonely Hearts Club Band* was released by Parlophone in Britain.

June 2: The LP *Sgt. Pepper's Lonely Hearts Club Band* was released in the U.S. by Capitol.

June: Paul McCartney revealed that he had taken LSD.

June 25: Forty million people in twenty-four countries watched the Beatles on the *Our World* TV program as they recorded "All You Need Is Love."

July 7: Parlophone released the group's fifteenth single, "All You Need Is Love" and "Baby, You're a Rich Man."

July 22: McCartney said that when they were told that *Our World* would be seen around the world, the group decided on "All You Need Is love," because love was the message that the world needed most.

July 24: The single "Baby, You're a Rich Man"/"All You Need Is Love" was released in the U.S. by Capitol.

A full page ad in the *Times* of London appeared, urging the abolition of marijuana laws. It was signed by all four Beatles, Brian Epstein, and other celebrities.

August 27: Brian Epstein was found dead. At the time the body was discovered, all four Beatles were at a transcendental meditation course in North Wales with the Marharishi Mahesh Yogi.

August 30: Clive Epstein, Brian's brother, moved up to become chairman of Nems. Robert Stigwood remained as managing director.

Brian Epstein was buried in Liverpool.

August 31: It was announced that the Beatles were to become their own managers.

September 11: The group began work on their upcoming movie, *Magical Mystery Tour*.

September: Frank Zappa announced that he agreed with Lennon's statement concerning Christ, and criticized Lennon for retracting it.

September: Lennon and Harrison appeared on David Frost's show, together with the Maharishi Mahesh Yogi, and they discussed transcendental meditation.

October 13: "How I Won the War" was released by United Artists, with some of Lennon's instrumentals heard on the recording.

October 18: The film *How I Won the War*, featuring John Lennon, premiered.

November 24: The Beatles' sixteenth single, "Hello Goodbye" and "I am the Walrus," was released in England by Parlophone.

November 27: The LP *Magical Mystery Tour* and the single "Hello Goodbye"/"I Am the Walrus" were released in the U.S. by Capitol.

December 1: The *Magical Mystery Tour* EP was released by Parlophone. The package contained two records, each with three songs, and a thirty-two-page cartoon book.

December 21: The group held another Christmas party, this time for their friends and for the *Magical Mystery Tour* staff.

December 26: The film *Medical Mystery Tour* was shown on the BBC in black and white. It was panned by the critics.

December 27: Paul McCartney defended *Magical Mystery Tour,* which he had directed, in an interview on the David Frost program on the BBC.

1968

January 6: It was reported that Epstein had left a fortune of almost 500,000 pounds sterling.

End of January: George Harrison spent ten days in Bombay composing and recording soundtrack music for his upcoming film *Wonderwall.*

February: Apple Corp., Ltd, was founded.

February 6: Ringo Starr was the guest star on Cilla Black's television show *Cilla* (U.K.).

February 17: It was announced by the English publisher Heinemann that the writer Hunter Davies had undertaken to write the official biography of the Beatles.

February 24: Paul McCartney stated that by setting up the business at Apple, the group was engaged in a kind of "Western Communism."

March-April: The entire group, their wives, and Jane Asher went to India to study with the Maharishi. They were joined there by Mia Farrow and also by Mike Love of the Beach Boys.

March 9: The LP *St. Pepper's Lonely Hearts Club Band* won four Grammy awards, for best album of the year, best contemporary album, best-engineered recording and best album cover.

March 15: The Beatles' seventeenth single was released by Parlophone, "Lady Madonna" and "The Inner Light" (the first song by George Harrison to be on a Beatles single). This was to be the last Beatles single released by Parlophone.

March 18: Capitol released the single "Lady Madonna"/"The Inner Light" in the U.S.

May 15: Lennon and McCartney, on a visit to the U.S. to promote Apple, appeared on the *Tonight* show.

May 22: In an interview while in the U.S., Lennon called the Vietnam War "insane."

June 15: John and Yoko planted two acorns at the Coventry Cathedral, and John said that they symbolized the East-West understanding that he and Yoko had achieved.

June 18: A one-act play based on Lennon's book *In His Own Write* opened at the National Theatre.

June 20: It was reported that the Beatles had reached agreement with both E.M.I. in Britain and Capitol in the United States that their future records would be distributed under the Apple label, and that those companies would distribute all Apple products for the next three years.

July 1: John and Yoko, both dressed in white, "plighted their troths" and released balloons to celebrate the event. Lennon said, "I declare the balloons high."

July 17: Ringo and Maureen, Paul, and John and Yoko attended the world premiere of *Yellow Submarine* at the London Pavilion.

July: Lennon and McCartney finished "Hey Jude."

July 13: All the stock of the Apple Boutique on Baker Street was given away to the crowd, at an estimated value of 20,000 pounds sterling. Pandemonium ensued.

August 11: National Apple Week was declared to launch Apple Records. The first record was "Thingumybob" by the Black Dyke Mills Band (conducted by Paul McCartney); George Harrison's *Wonderwall* LP was also released.

August 16: "Those Were the Days," by Mary Hopkin and produced by McCartney, was released by Apple. The record went on to sell 4 million copies within four months.

August 23: It was reported that Cynthia Lennon was suing for divorce, citing Yoko Ono as the reason.

August 26: The Beatles' eighteenth single, "Hey Jude"/"Revolution," was released in the United States by Apple.

August 30: The single "Hey Jude"/"Revolution" was released in the U.S. on the Apple label—the first Beatles' record to be released on the label there.

September 8: The group appeared on the *Frost on Sunday* show, on London Weekend TV, and performed "Hey Jude."

September 14: The official biography of the Beatles, by Hunter Davies, was published by Heinemann. On the same day it was reported that "Hey Jude" had already grossed sales of 2 million copies. That evening, a documentary called *All My Loving* was aired on British television.

October 6: George Harrison made a surprise appearance on the *Smothers Brothers Comedy Hour* to promote "Hey Jude."

October 18: British police raided John and Yoko's apartment in Marylebone, and arrested them on the charge of possession of marijuana. Later that day, they were released on bail.

October 28: Cynthia Lennon officially filed for her divorce petition.

November 8: John and Yoko took an advertisement in the music journals advocating support for the "Peace Ship." This was an independent radio station that broadcast peaceful messages to the disputing sides in the Middle East.

Cynthia Lennon received her divorce.

November 9: The LP *Unfinished Music No. 1—Two Virgins* was released by Apple, featuring John and Yoko nude on the cover.

November 21: Yoko Ono had a miscarriage while in the hospital in London. John Lennon remained by her side throughout.

November 25: The Beatles (known as the White Album) was released in the United States, on the Apple label.

November 28: The *Yellow Submarine* LP was released by Apple in Great Britain.

Lennon admitted possession of cannabis resin, and was fined 150 pounds sterling. Yoko, who had just lost her baby, was not involved in any legal action.

November 30: Apple released *The Beatles* (known as the White Album) in Britain. On the same day it was reported that sales of "Hey Jude" had reached 6 million worldwide.

December 18: John Lennon and Yoko Ono appeared at Albert Hall, in London, writhing on stage in a large white bag.

End of December: The film *Rape* was produced by John Lennon and Yoko Ono for Austrian television.

December: Filmings for John and Yoko Ono's *Rock 'n' Roll Circus* was done, but the movie was never commercially released.

1969

January: Work began on *Let It Be.*

January 3: Thousands of *Two Virgins* LPs, with photos of John and Yoko nude, were seized in New Jersey as pornographic material.

January 13: The LP *Yellow Submarine* was released in the United States by Apple.

January 30: The Beatles gave their last public concert, on top of the Apple Building, at 3 Saville Row, London.

February 23: Paul McCartney introduced Mary Hopkin on the *David Frost Show* in the United States.

March 7: John and Yoko gave a concert at Cambridge, England.

March 12: Paul McCartney and Linda Eastman were married at the Marylebone register office. On that same day, George Harrison's home was raided by police, when only his wife Patti was home. When he returned home, they both were arrested, and then later released on bail.

March: ATV announced its intention to buy a controlling share of Northern Songs and to that end purchased all of Dick James's shares in the company.

March 20: While on vacation in Paris, John and Yoko made a day trip to Gibraltar and got married, with two executives from Apple, Peter Brown and David Nuttall, as their witnesses.

March 21: Allen Klein, it was announced, had been appointed to a three-year contract as business manager for the Beatles and their company, Apple.

March 26: John and Yoko demonstrated for peace by staying in their bed for seven days, at the Amsterdam Hilton, where they were honeymooning.

March 31: George Harrison and his wife Patti were fined 250 pounds sterling each for possession of marijuana.

April 1: At a press conference held in Vienna the day following the premiere of their film *Rape,* John and Yoko were dressed in oversized white pillow cases, and talked about love and peace to reporters. On the same day Lennon, saying that he was nearly broke, announced that he was going back to work recording with the Beatles, and also that he was sending two acorns to each of the world's leaders so that they could plant a seed for peace.

April 5: Dick James, the managing director of Northern Songs, was reported to have failed to persuade Paul McCartney and John Lennon to accept ATV's offer of 9 million pounds sterling for the company.

April 10: The Beatles officially rejected an offer made by ATV and announced their intention to acquire ATV's 35 percent share in the company.

April 18: The group's nineteenth single, "Get Back" and "Don't Let Me Down," was released by Apple, in Britain. "Don't Let Me Down" featured Billy Preston on the piano, the first time another artist had appeared on one of the Beatles' singles.

April 25: The Beatles offered a total of 2.1 million pounds sterling for the 20 percent of the shares they would need to control Northern Songs.

April 26: In an official ceremony held on the roof of the Apple building, John Winston Lennon changed his middle name to Ono.

May 1: The LP *Unfinished Music No. 2—Life with the Lions* was released in the U.K. by Apple, for John and Yoko on their new Zapple label. One of the tracks was a recording of the heartbeat of the baby that Yoko had eventually miscarried.

May 3: George Harrison's LP *Electronic Sounds* was released by Apple, on its new Zapple label, in Britain.

May 4: Ringo Starr and Peter Sellers threw a party to celebrate the completion of the film *The Magic Christian*. John and Yoko attended, as did Paul and Linda McCartney, as well as a host of other British and American stars.

May 5: It was reported that John and Yoko had bought Tittenhurst Park, Ascot, a mansion with grounds of 72 acres. On the same day, the single "Get Back"/"Don't Let Me Down" was released by Apple in the U.S.

May 19: Once again, Lennon and McCartney received the Ivor Novello award for top-selling song in Britain during 1968.

May 20: The Beatles' twentieth single—and the last one recorded by Lennon and McCartney together—was released by Apple: "The Ballad of John and Yoko" and "Old Brown Shoe."

May 26: Apple records released John Lennon's *Unfinished Music No. 2—Life with the Lions* on the Zapple label, in the U.S.

June 16: The single "The Ballad of John and Yoko" and "Old Brown Shoe" was released in the U.S. by Apple.

July 28: Apple released the John Lennon and the Plastic Ono Band single "Give Peace a Chance" and "Remember Love" in Britain and in the U.S.

End of July: John, Yoko, and Kyoko (Yoko's daughter) were injured in a car accident in Scotland.

September: Wedding Album, an LP by John and Yoko, complete with photos of John and Yoko's wedding, was released by Apple in Britain.

London's New Cinema Club held "An Evening With John and Yoko," and featured four of their films.

It was reported that ATV had purchased nearly 50 percent of Northern Songs in their attempt to gain control of the company.

September 13: John Lennon and the Plastic Ono Band held a Rock and Roll Revival Concert in Varsity Stadium, Toronto.

September 26: Abbey Road was released in Britain by Apple.

October 1: "Abbey Road" was released in the United States by Apple.

October: Lennon was reported to have complained about the waste and inefficiency of Apple, saying that most of the nonrecording ventures were failures. Also during that month, John Lennon ahd the Plastic Ono Band released the single "Cold Turkey"/"Don't Worry Kyoko" through Apple, in the U.K. Eric Clapton played the guitar.

"Paul is dead" rumors began to grow, prompted by *Abby Road* jacket design.

October 13: The Beatles' single "Something"/"Come Together" was released in the U.S. by Apple.

October 16: It was announced that the Beatles had agreed to sell all their shares in Northern Songs to ATV at a price determined through arbitration.

October 20: The LP Wedding Album, done by John and Yoko, was released in the U.S. by Apple.

November 9: Reports circulated that John and Yoko had made a film of themselves floating through the sky in a hot-air balloon. The film was called *Apotheosis.*

November 10: The John Lennon and the Plastic Ono Band single "Cold Turkey"/"Don't Worry Kyoko" was released in the U.S. by Apple.

November 25: Lennon returned his M.B.E. to Queen Elizabeth, with love, but as a protest against support of U.S. policy in Vietnam, and also against British policy toward the war in Biafra.

December: John Lennon released the LP *The Plastic Ono Band—Live Peace in Toronto* in the U.K. on the Apple label. Eric Clapton played the guitar.

December 15: Lennon's *The Plastic Ono Band—Live Peace In Toronto* was released by Apple in the U.S.

1970

February 23: The *Hey Jude* LP was released in the United States by Apple. On that same day, Ringo appeared in a few skits on Rowan and Martin's *Laugh-in* television show.

March 2: Lennon's single "Instant Karma"/"Who Has Seen the Wind?" was released in the United States by Apple.

March 16: The Beatles' single "Let It Be"/"You Know My Name" was released in the U.S. on Apple.

April: Apple released Paul McCartney's first solo album, *McCartney,* and also Ringo Starr's solo album *"Sentimental Journey,* in Britain and in the U.S.

April 9: Paul McCartney appeared on *London Weekend* TV.

April 10: Apple press officer Derek Taylor announced that Paul McCartney had left the Beatles because of "personal, business, and musical differences."

May 8: The LP *Let It Be* was released by Apple, in Britain.

May 14: The film *Let It Be* premiered in New York.

May 18: The LP *Let It Be* was released in New York by Apple.

May 20: The film *Let It Be* premiered in both London and Liverpool, but none of the Beatles attended.

May 25: The single "The Long and Winding Road"/ "For You Blue" was released in the U.S. by Apple. It was later reported that the record sold 1.2 million copies in two days.

May: The *McCartney* solo LP was reported to have sold over 1 million copies in four weeks, and Ringo's *Sentimental Journey* was reported to have sold over 500,000 copies in two weeks.

August 1: Cynthia Lennon and Roberto Bassanini, an Italian hotel owner, were married.

September 22: John and Yoko were guests on the *Dick Cavett Show* in the U.S.

September 28: Lennon and McCartney jointly sued Northern Songs for half of all the money the company had received.

December 9: John Lennon released the LP *The Plastic Ono Band* on Apple in Britain and in the United States.

December 31: Paul McCartney initiated legal proceedings to end the business partnership of the Beatles.

1971

January 4: The single "Mother"/"Why" was released by Lennon, through Apple in Britain and the U.S.

February: The lawsuit initiated by McCartney went before the High Court, where he was opposed by the three other Beatles, Allen Klein, and Apple Corp., Ltd.

March 5: "Power to the People" and "Open Your Box" were released by John Lennon and the Plastic Ono Band in the U.K. on the Apple label.

March 12: The High Court appointed a receiver to handle the Beatles' assets, and also enjoined Allen Klein from any further role in the management of the group's affairs.

March 19: John, George, and Ringo appealed against the appointment of a receiver.

April 29 The single "Power to the People"/"Touch Me" was released by Apple in the United States.

May 15: The Filmmaker's Fortnight Festival in Cannes, France, featured two films done by John and Yoko *Apotheosis* (*Balloon*) and *Fly.*

June 6: Frank Zappa, John, and Yoko played together on the stage of the Fillmore East, in New York City.

August 1: The Bangla Desh Concert was held at Madison Square Garden in New York City, with Ringo Starr, George Harrison, Eric Clapton, Ravi Shankar, Bob Dylan, Badfinger, Leon Russell, and others participating.

August: John and Yoko moved to New York City.

September: The LP *Imagine* was released by Lennon on the Apple label in Britain.

October 4: The single "Imgine"/"It's So Hard" was released in the U.S. by Lennon on Apple.

December 6: The single "Happy Xmas (War Is Over)"/"Listen, the Snow Is Fallin" was released in the U.S. by Lennon, on the Apple label.

December 11: John and Yoko performed at a benefit for John Sinclair in Ann Arbor, Michigan.

1972

January 13: John and Yoko were guests on the *David Frost Show* in the U.S.

February: The BBC banned the single done by Paul McCartney and the Wings entitled "Give Ireland Back to the Irish (Parts 1 and 2)," which was released throughout the United Kingdom by Apple.

February 21-25: John and Yoko cohosted the *Mike Douglas Show* for a week, on New York TV. During that week, they played a session with Chuck Berry.

February 29: Lennon's visa expired, but he continued to stay in New York, to search for Yoko's child Kyoko. The U.S. government refused to grant Lennon permission to stay, however, and his battle with immigration authorities began.

March 23: The Concert for Bangla Desh movie premiered.

April 4: John and Yoko were guests on the *Dick Cavett* Show.

May 8: John and Yoko released the single "Woman Is the Nigger Of the World"/"Sisters, O Sisters" in both Britain and the U.S. on Apple.

May 11: John and Yoko guested on the *Dick Cavett Show.*
   The television special *John and Yoko in Syracuse, N.Y.,* taped from Yoko's exhibit at the Everson Museum, was broadcast.

June 19: John Lennon released the LP *Some Time in New York City* on the Apple label.

August 31: John and Yoko headlined on "One-to-One," a benefit concert for mentally retarded children held at Madison Square Garden, New York.

December 15: A film of the "One-to-One" concert was shown on television in the U.S.

December 23: John and Yoko's new movie *Imagine* premiered.

1973

March: The U.S. immigration bureau sent down an order for John Lennon's deportation, on the grounds of his drug conviction in 1968.

March 8: Paul McCartney was fined 100 pounds sterling for growing marijuana on his farm.

April 2: Two new collections of Beatles songs, the LPs *"The Beatles 1962-1966* and *The Beatles 1967-1970,* were released by Apple in the U.K.

July 10: John, George, and Ringo recorded together for the first time in four years when they did John's "I'm the Greatest" for the *Ringo* album.

October: John separated from Yoko and moved to Los Angeles.

October 22: The Lennon single "Mind Games"/"Meat City" was released by Apple.

October 30: The LP *Mind Games* was released by Lennon on the Apple label.

1974

February 25: A spokesman for the receiver of the Beatles' financial interests indicated that some resolution of the dilemma was near. However, it was also reported that it would be necessary for the four of them to be contractually bound until 1976.

May 25: It was reported that George Harrison had formed his own label, Dark Horse Records, and further, that he had signed a worldwide distribution deal with AMI Records.

July 26: In Boston, two thousand fans attended a Beatles Appreciation Convention and then demonstrated against the deportation order served on John Lennon. A few months later, a similar event was held in New York, to which John donated a guitar to be auctioned off for charity.

August 15: A play entitled *John, Paul, George, Ringo, and Bert,* written by Willy Russell, a teacher from Liverpool, opened in London.

August 31: In New York federal court, John Lennon claimed that the Nixon administration tried to have him deported because he had helped to organize an antiwar demonstration at the Republican National Convention in 1972. Lennon also claimed that his phone had been tapped illegally. Of his conviction for possession of marijuana in 1968, Lennon commented that he had thought that it would have been forgotten by then.

September 13: "Many Rivers to Cross" was released by Harry Nilsson. The song was arranged and produced by Lennon, and it was taken from the LP *Pussy Cats,* on which the two had worked together.

September 23: "Whatever Gets You Thru the Night"/ "Beef Jerky," Lennon's single, was released in the U.S. by Apple. Elton John played organ and piano, and sang on the title track.

September 26: John Lennon's LP *Wall and Bridges* was released in the United States on Apple.

October 4: The LP *Walls and Bridges* and the single "Whatever Gets You Thru the Night"/"Beef Jerky" were released in Britain under the Apple label.

November 14: The *Sgt. Pepper's Lonely Hearts Club Band on the Road* stage show hit New York; Lennon appeared at a press conference to promote it.

November: The LP *Goodnight Vienna* was released on the Apple label by Ringo Starr. The title song was written by Lennon, and he also appeared on the album.

November: Elton John's version of "Lucy in the Sky with Diamonds" was released, and it featured John Lennon.

November 28: Elton John and John Lennon appeared together on the stage of Madison Square Garden in New York and sang "Whatever Gets You Thru the Night," "I Saw Her Standing There," and "Lucy in the Sky with Diamonds."

December 13: George Harrison and his father visited the White House, at the invitation of President Ford's son Jack. Harrison reported "good vibes."

December 16: It was reported that as president, Richard Nixon had ordered the harassment and deportation of John Lennon.

Lennon's single "No. 9 Dream"/"What You Got" was released by Apple.

1975

January 9: The last legal links between the Beatles were dissolved in court.

February 17: John Lennon released the LP *Rock 'n' Roll* under the Apple label. The album featured songs sung in the Beatles' early days in Hamburg.

March 1: John Lennon was a guest presenter on the *Grammy Awards* show.

March 10: The single "Stand by Me"/"Move Over Ms. L" was released by Apple.

March: John Lennon returned from Los Angeles and rejoined Yoko in New York City.

April 28: John guested on the *Tomorrow* show.

May 21: The Beatles Special with David Frost was aired in the U.S.

June 13: John performed in the television show *Salute to Lew Grade* in the U.S.

October 9: After three miscarriages during the course of their relationship, a boy, Sean Ono, was born to John and Yoko Lennon.

October 22: The LP *Shaved Fish* was released by Lennon on the Apple label.

1976

May 31: The single "Got to Get You into My Life"/"Helter Skelter" was issued by Capitol.

June 11: Rock and Roll Music, an LP, was released. This collection of classic Beatles songs was backed by one of the largest promotional campaigns in the history of the business, by Parlophone in Britain and Capitol in the U.S.

July 27: The U.S. government dropped its efforts to deport John Lennon and granted him a green card—permanent resident alien status. Lennon commented: "As usual, there is a great woman behind every idiot."

November 1: "Ob-La-Di; Ob-La-Da" was released as a single by Apple.

1977

April: Beatlemania, a Broadway musical, opened at the Winter Garden Theatre in New York. Beatle lookalike musicians played Beatles songs against a background of film clips from the 1960s. Although the show opened for a limited engagement, it ran for three years on Broadway, and also had a very successful tour. In 1979, it was reported that an agent for the Beatles had sued the producers of *Beatlemania* for unauthorized use of the Beatles' material.

May: John and Yoko went to Japan to show their son, Sean Ono, to Yoko's parents. John had prepared for the trip by studying Japanese.

May 1: The LP *The Beatles at Hollywood Bowl,* the first official live Beatles album, was released by Parlophone in Britain and Capitol in the United States. The album contained some recordings that had never before been released.

October 24: The LP *Love Songs* was released by Parlophone in Britain and Capitol in the United States. A book of lyrics accompanied this collection of old Beatles love songs.

1978

February 19: A television special about the Beatles, *All You Need Is Love,* was shown in the United States.

August 14: The Beatles single "Sgt. Pepper's Lonely Hearts Club Band"/"With a Little Help from My Friends"/"A Day in the Life" was released by Parlophone in Britain and Capitol in the United States.

1979

May 27: The following open letter was run as a paid advertisement in the Sunday editions of newspapers in New York, London, and Tokyo:

A LOVE LETTER FROM
JOHN AND YOKO TO PEOPLE WHO ASK
US WHAT, WHEN, AND WHY

The past ten years we noticed everything we wished came true in its own time, good or bad, one way or the other. We kept telling each other that one of these days we would have to get organized and wish for only good things. Then our baby arrived! We were over-joyed and at the same time felt very responsible. Now our wishes would also affect *him*. We felt it was time for us to stop discussing and do something about our wishing process: The Spring Cleaning of our minds! It was a lot of work. We kept finding things in those old closets in our minds that we hadn't realized were still there, things we wished we hadn't found. As we did our cleaning, we also started to notice many wrong things in our house: there was a shelf which should have never been there in the first place, a painting we grew to dislike, and there were the two dingy rooms, which became light and breezy when we broke the walls between them. We started to love the plants, which one of us originally thought were robbing the air from us! We began to enjoy the drum beat of the city which used to annoy us. We made a lot of mistakes and still do. In the past we spent a lot of energy in trying to get something we thought we wanted, won-dered why we didn't get it, only to find out that one or both of us didn't really want it. One day, we received a sudden rain of chocolates from people around the world. "Hey, what's this! We're not eating sugar stuff, are we?" "Who's wishing it?" We both laughed. We discovered that when two off us wished in unison, it happened faster. As the Good Book says—Where two are gathered together—It's true. Two is plenty. A Newclear Seed.

More and more we are starting to wish and pray. The things we have tried to achieve in the past by flashing a V sign, we try now through wishing. We are not doing this because it is simpler. Wishing is more effective than waving flags. It works. It's like magic. Magic is simple. Magic is real. The secret of it is to know that it is simple, and not kill it with an elaborate ritual which is a sign of insecurity. When somebody is angry with us, we draw a halo around his or her head in our minds. Does the person stop being angry then? Well, we don't know! We know, though, that when we draw a halo around a person, suddenly the person starts to look like an angel to us. This helps us to feel warm toward the person, reminds us that everyone has goodness inside, and that all people who come to us are angels in disguise, carrying messages and gifts to use from the Universe. Magic is logical. Try it sometime.

We still have a long way to go. It seems the more we get into cleaning, the faster the wishing and receiving process gets. The house is getting very comfortable now. Sean is beautiful. The plants are growing. The cats are purring. The town is shining, sun, rain, or snow. We live in a beautiful universe. We are thankful every day for the plentifulness of our life. This is not a euphemism. We understand that we, the city, the country, the earth are facing very hard times, and there is panic in the air. Still the sun is shining and we are here together, and there is love between us, our city, the country, the earth. If two people like us can do what we are doing with our lives, any miracle is possible! It's true we can do with a few big miracles right now. The thing is to recognize them when they come to you and be thankful. First they come in a small way, in everyday life, then they come in rivers, and in oceans. It's goin' to be all right! The future of the earth is up to all of us.

Many people are sending us vibes every day in letters, telegrams, taps on the gate, or just flowers and nice thoughts. We thank them all and appreciate them for respecting our quiet space, which we need. Thank you for all the love you send us. We feel it every day. We love you, too. We know you are concerned about us. That is nice. That's why you want to know what we are doing. That's why everybody is asking us What, When, and Why. We understand. Well, this is what we've been doing. We hope that you have the same quiet space in your mind to make your own wishes come true.

If you think of us next time, remember, our silence is a silence of love and not of indifference. Remember, we are writing in the sky instead of on paper—that's our song. Lift your eyes and look up in the sky. There's our message. Lift your eyes again and look around you, and you will see that you are walking in the sky, which extends to the ground. We are all part of the sky, more so than of the ground. Remember, we love you.

> John and Yoko Ono
> May 27, 1979
> New York City

P.S. We noticed that three angels were looking over our shoulders when we wrote this!

1980

March 24: The Beatles Rarities was released in the U.S. by Capitol Records.

July: John Lennon and a five-man crew sailed from Newport to Bermuda on a friend's yacht.

November: Lennon's LP *Double Fantasy* was released by Lennon Music, Inc.

December 6: Mark David Chapman arrived in New York from Honolulu.

December 8: Mark Chapman shot John Lennon four times, killing him.

December 14: A ten-minute silent vigil was held to commemorate Lennon's death.

ABOUT THE AUTHORS

VIC GARBARINI is Managing Editor of *Musician: Player & Listener* Magazine.

BRIAN CULLMAN is the leader of the band Second Thoughts and is a regular columnist for *Musician: Player & Listener* Magazine.

BARBARA GRAUSTARK is presently an Associate Editor of *Newsweek* Magazine and in September 1980 conducted the first interview with John Lennon and Yoko Ono in five years.

In keeping with the Lennons' ideals, the authors of this book will donate a portion of their earnings to various charities.